PEKING
TABLE TOP
COOKING

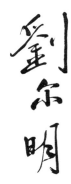

Linda Lew   Agnes Lee
&
Elizabeth Brotherton

Interior Illustrations by Joe Brotherton

GALA BOOKS
4444 Vineland Avenue
North Hollywood, California 91603

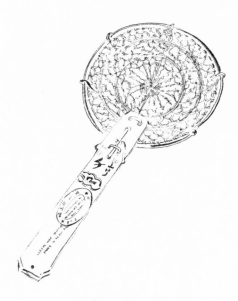

Library of Congress Catalog Number: 72-86537
ISBN Number: 0-912448-06-7
© Copyright 1972 by Gala Books
Composed and Printed in the United States of America

TABLE OF CONTENTS

They say there is
no end to it

PEKING KITCHEN

Peking food is the most delicious, varied, and elegant in the world. Classic Mandarin delicacies and the hearty dumplings of the street vendors, both are characteristic of this ancient Northern city. Many styles of food from the provinces are found here—the spicy succulent sauces from the province of Szechwan, and the light fresh vegetables from the province of Kwangtung—each valued for its special tastes.

We Americans have known Chinese food best in the style of the city of Canton in South China, because most Chinese restaurants here are Cantonese. The cooking of North China is different: basically, it uses more pastries and breads, and less rice; more richly spiced things and less bland vegetables; it is more savory and less sweet. The materials are those native to a cold climate, and the flavors are lively and robust.

Can these flavors be produced in an American kitchen? I thought I should ask a Chinese woman rather than a restaurant chef, because her problems are like mine: how to eat well with little money, how to vary seasonings and enjoy cooking, how to cook for friends without making a frantic fuss about it. How does she cope, that clever Chinese housewife? What does she choose of the American abundance; and how does she produce those incomparable Chinese flavors?

In my effort to learn what I could from Chinese who have adapted their cuisine to American surroundings, I studied cooking with Linda Lew. Linda could teach me a good deal about adapting: she grew up in Chungking, raised children in Taipei, and now lives and teaches Chinese cooking in San Francisco. Her tastes remain firmly attached to the sturdy cuisine of North China and the lively spices of Szechwan—which are much admired in Peking. She studied cooking in Taipei, that melting pot of so many Chinese styles. The recipes in this book are Linda's and her daughter Agnes'.

All recipes are sufficient for six people—providing several dishes are served at one meal, which is the custom in Chinese dining.

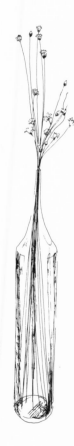

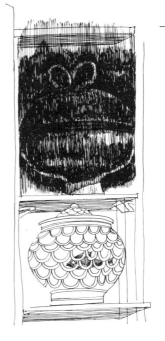

CHINESE
INGREDIENTS

The first lesson in Peking cooking is to learn the basic cooking ingredients and flavorings. Many are exotic to Western tastes, others are as familiar as water chestnuts. All these ingredients are available in Oriental markets and many are becoming increasingly available in supermarkets.

This introduction also covers useful Chinese cooking utensils, staples to keep on hand in the cupboard and refrigerator, time-saving tips on preparing and freezing ingredients for future use, and basic recipes for Chinese rice & Basic Sauce.

Bamboo shoot. A crisp, lightly-flavored vegetable, cone-shaped, about 6 inches long. Generally sliced fine in 1/4 inch strips for stir-fried dishes. Sold fresh in some Oriental markets and sold canned in most supermarkets. Fresh bamboo shoots must be boiled 1/2 hour; if canned they need only a few minutes cooking. They keep well for a week if refrigerated. Substitute: any crisp, mild-tasting vegetable.

Bean cake is the white curd of soybean milk, sold in 3 inch squares about 3/4 inch thick. It is bland in flavor, so it should be cooked in a tasty sauce, or stuffed with spicy meat filling, or deep fried, or sauteed in matchstick strips. It is worthwhile to learn the several methods of preparing bean cake. It's loaded with protein high in quality but low in cost—a wonderful combination; so seek it out, fresh or canned, at any Oriental food store.

Bean cake keeps for at least a week in water in the refrigerator. For most ways of cooking it, it's helpful to dry and solidify it slightly. To do this, lay it one layer deep on a paper towel on a plate; put another paper towel over it, and another plate inverted over that. Put this arrangement in the refrigerator and weigh it down slightly with another plate. Turn it all over after a day or two.

Bean cake may be kept outside the refrigerator for a week if it is cubed and pan-fried lightly with salt.

Bean threads are peastarch noodles, sometimes called vermicelli, cellophane noodles, or long rice. They are a starchy addition to soups, stews, or the hot pot; their flavor is very mild. To prepare them, pour boiling water over them, soak for 30 minutes. Sold dried in Oriental markets and some supermarkets. Substitutes: fine vermicelli, rice vermicelli.

Black beans are salted, fermented soybeans. Used most frequently with shellfish, but also with other meat and fish. Sold in Chinese markets in plastic bags. They are moist, but they keep well without refrigeration if tightly covered. To make a black bean sauce, soak them for 20 minutes, then mash them, adding an equal volume of water or broth.

Chinese parsley. Green leaves of the coriander plant. With its strong, aromatic flavor and fragrance, it is used to garnish soups, salads, and chicken stir-fried dishes. Use the leaves only. It is sold fresh in Chinese, Puerto Rican, and Mexican markets, and many supermarkets (in Spanish it is called cilantro). Its flavor has no substitute; if you don't have it, use minced chives or celery tops for garnish. The coriander herb is easily grown: try raising your own in a flower pot on a windowsill.

Clouds' ears. A small, ruffled tree mushroom, valued for its springy, chewy consistency. Sold dried in Chinese markets, it comes in black or white—presumably depending on which side of the tree it grew. The white is much more expensive, but if this is due to the difference in flavor, the distinction escapes all but the most perceptive.

Like other dried mushrooms, they must be soaked: put them in a bowl and pour hot water from the tap over them. Soak for 20 minutes, and squeeze to remove any sand still clinging to them.

Then they may be cooked with vegetables; or, steamed with sugar for breakfast or dessert.

Ginger root is an important flavor-changer, used in cooking all seafood and most fresh meat. It makes fish less fishy without diminishing the delicate seafood taste; and it modifies raw and harsh flavors in meat. To prepare it, cut cross-wise a 1/8 inch slice of the root and mince it; or, give it a slap with the flat of your cleaver to crush it. If fresh ginger root is not obtainable, then preserved ginger root may be substituted.

You can avoid last minute chopping and cutting in the preparation of ginger root if you make ginger juice ahead of time. Store it with your soy sauce and cornstarch for ready access when you start cooking.

GINGER JUICE
1/2 cup ginger root, sliced finely across
    the grain
1 cup thin soy sauce
2 Tbsp wine, Kao Liang

Spin ginger root and soy sauce together in blendor until smooth. Pour into a small storage jar with a tight-fitting lid. Add wine. Stir the contents from the bottom when you use it.

Hot oil is peanut oil spiced with chili peppers. Used as a flavoring, it provides zest and heat—but lightly. Spiciness from the oil does not permeate the food, but gives a lively aftertaste. Hot oil may be purchased, or made at home:

HOT OIL
2 cups peanut oil
2 oz dried Jalapeño (chili) peppers
Heat oil until it starts to smoke, turn off the heat, add peppers, let them stand overnight, strain.

Hot Chili Paste can be purchased in Oriental markets, and it is even stronger than hot oil. If a recipe says, 1 tsp hot oil, and you wish to substitute hot paste, then add only 1/4 tsp hot paste—cautiously—and taste as you go. Both hot oil and hot chili paste keep indefinitely without refrigeration.

Jellyfish. A form of marine life; white, flat, without flavor, of a chewy consistency. May be sliced and eaten alone as hors d'oeuvre, or added to salad. It is sold salty and moist in plastic bags. Put it in a bowl and pour hot water from the tap over it, let it stand for 1 hour, rinse and slice. Keeps in the refrigerator for 2 weeks or more.

Mushrooms. Dried, imported Chinese mushrooms are very tasty. Soak them before cooking, in 1/2 cup hot water for 20 minutes, and squeeze them out to release any sand in them. The sand sinks to the bottom of the bowl, and you can then pour the soaking water out carefully to use for broth.

Preserved pepper. Fresh red chili or Jalapena peppers in brine with wine. To use, chop and add them to stir-fried dishes at any time in the cooking process. They lend both spice and color. Make your own, for the best flavor, and put them in a small, ornamental jar to decorate your basket of Chinese ingredients: they are remarkably handsome.

PRESERVED PEPPER

1/2 cup salt
2 cups water
1/2 lb fresh red Jalapeño (chili) peppers
1/2 cup Kao Liang wine

Boil the salt and water together and let it cool. Wash the peppers and dry them carefully. Cut off the stem end and make 3 slits down the end about 1/2 inch. Pack lightly in a glass jar that can be covered, then pour the salt water over them, leaving 1/5 of the space at the top of the jar to add wine. Set them aside in a cool place or in the refrigerator to mature for two months.

These peppers will keep indefinitely, and you may keep adding more peppers, boiled brine and wine as you deplete the jar. They must remain uncontaminated by either fresh water or oil, however, so remember to wash and dry the peppers before adding them to your storage jar.

For a substitute, pickled Chilies Jalapeños have the right flavor but lack the rich, fiery color of the fresh peppers.

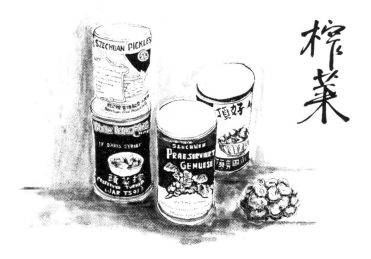

Preserved turnip. The bulbous stem of a mustard plant, pickled, canned, and imported from China. It may be eaten sliced as an hors d'oeuvre, by those who have learned to like its pungent, salty taste by itself. It's most useful for its very lively piquancy that blends and enlivens all other flavors, but does not stand out by itself to affront conservative Western palates. It's indispensable minced in chow mein and other stir-fry dishes. It is variously called Pickled Mustard Green Stems, Szechwan Mustard Pickles, Szechuen Preserved Vegetable, Chinese Radish, and (in Chinese) Cha Ts'ai.

Preserved turnip keeps indefinitely in the refrigerator. Remove it from the can, and do not wash off the residue of red chili pepper that clings to it.

Effort spent in obtaining this exotic vegetable is amply rewarded.

Seaweed. Dried purple seaweed used in soup, is sold in flat sheets about 8 inches square. Like dried mushrooms and dried shrimp, it may have sand on it, so be sure to soak it. Put it in a bowl, pour about 1/2 cup hot water over it, let it soak several minutes. Stir it gently, while soaking, to let any sand settle to the bottom of the bowl. Strain the seaweed, and add the soaking water to the broth. (Pour it out very carefully; the sand will remain in the bottom of soaking bowl.)

Sesame oil, pressed from roasted sesame seeds, has a rich, nutlike flavor. The flavor dissipates quickly, however, so sesame oil is generally added when cooking is nearly finished. It is sold at Oriental markets, Middle Eastern markets and some supermarkets. It keeps well without refrigeration.

Sesame seeds also are widely available. You can buy them already roasted, or roast them at home this way: Wash and cull them. Heat them for about 10 minutes in a dry frying pan over moderate heat. Stir frequently. Brown lightly; do not burn, or they'll be bitter.

Shrimp. Dried, peeled shrimp are added as a distinctive, salty flavoring to ground meat and soups. Soak shrimp for 20 minutes in hot water, and then mince.

Soy sauce is a salty, thin, brown liquid, used to marinate almost all fish and meat; and also flavors sauces and stews. It comes in two main types, Thin and Dark. Dark (or Black) soy sauce is rather sweet, and is favored by Cantonese Chinese. Thin soy sauce is salty, lighter in color, and preferred by cooks in Northern provinces. Recipes in this book call for Thin soy sauce unless indicated otherwise. The well known Kikkoman soy sauce, for example, falls between Dark and Thin. It will do, however, if you cannot obtain Thin soy sauce. Please note: soy sauce and salt are not interchangeable.

Star anise is a dried, brown seed-pod; eight-lobed, about 1 inch in diameter. Put it directly into sauces and stews to enrich the flavor. Its heavy licorice character is evident in Tea Eggs. Substitute: aniseed.

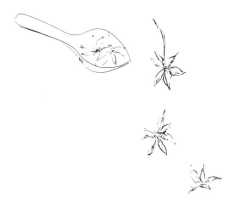

Sweet rice, or glutinous rice, is short-grained rice used for poultry stuffing, pastries, and sweet congee. It should be soaked overnight (or in warm water for 2 or 3 hours) before cooking, and then drained. To cook it, place it on a dampened paper towel in a steamer. It takes longer to cook than long-grained rice, and it is sticky. Sweet rice powder is commonly used in desserts.

Szechwan pepper is also called wild pepper, or Hua Chiao; or, in Cantonese stores, far pepper. It belies its name, for Szechwan pepper has a bland, indescribable taste that nicely complements and brings out other flavors. It's an excellent topper sprinkled on a dish at the last moment. It looks like the red-brown husks of peppercorns. To prepare it: pick out and discard the few peppercorn centers that are still intact. Then roast in a dry frying pan over moderate heat for the few minutes until it pops. Pulverize it in a mortar, and store for ready access. You may mix it with salt and have a two-in-one seasoning.

Tangerine peel. Used to flavor chicken, bean soup. Dried, imported. Soak it in water overnight or longer and slice it in 1/4 inch wide strips. For tangerine chicken, mix the slices with soy sauce and let it stand for a few days or a week before adding to the chicken. Substitute: grated peeling from a fresh orange.

Vinegar. Rice vinegar is the kind to use here—either white, red, or black. All are mild and smooth. (When something is too salty, add a little vinegar.) Sold in Oriental markets. White wine vinegar will do as a substitute.

Water chestnut. A root vegetable, walnut-sized, used for its delicately crisp texture. Slice, and add it to meat fillings or stir-

fried dishes. Sold canned or fresh. If it is fresh, simmer it whole for 10 minutes, cool, and peel it with your fingers. To store surplus canned water chestnuts, cover with water in a refrigerator jar. Substitute: jicama, celery, or any crisp vegetable.

Wine. Of the many Chinese wines, Kao Liang is the type most useful in the kitchen. Kao Liang is really a distillate of millet; clear, powerful (100 proof) and more like Western gin or vodka than like Western grape wine. It enhances and preserves the flavor of most seafoods and meat. To use it as a preservative for meat, combine a tablespoonful, with 1/4 cup soy sauce, and pour over sliced meat. The meat will keep in the refrigerator for as long as a week before you cook it. Kao Liang is also used as a preservative in making that most useful concoction of the kitchen: ginger juice. It's also used in garlic juice, and preserved peppers. Substitute: gin in the ginger juice, garlic juice, or preserved peppers; and gin or sherry for cooking meat and seafood.

EIGHT CHINESE FLAVORINGS

Eight Chinese flavorings improve, change, or increase the flavor of foods. Most of these can be obtained at Chinese grocery stores, many at Japanese markets or gourmet stores, and some are now found at supermarkets. There are many other flavorings, and one of the joys of cooking is discovering and experimenting with new ones. If you have these eight, however, you can cook most of the recipes in this book; and in fact, most Chinese dishes.

ginger root (or ginger juice)	soy sauce
hot oil (or hot paste)	star anise
rice vinegar	Szechwan pepper
sesame oil	Chinese wine

All of these ingredients keep indefinitely, and do not need refrigeration, except for fresh ginger root which, nevertheless, lasts for many days.

Put all the flavorings together with a box of cornstarch and a box of salt on a small tray. Then you can conveniently pull them out of the cupboard at once when you prepare to cook.

White Sesame
or
Pepper
Roasting Pan
&
Paddle

AMERICAN INGREDIENTS
FOR
A CHINESE KITCHEN

American ingredients for Oriental cooking must be carefully chosen in order to recreate the famous flavors of China.

Generally, the meat used most often is fresh pork. A boneless Boston butt is the best cut, because it is sufficiently fat, both for ground pork and for stir-fried pork slices. If possible, have the butcher grind it to order. Of beef cuts, the flank steak is most convenient. Ham is used if a very high grade can be purchased; the Italian prosciutto is like a China ham, and an American Smithfield ham is much prized. In meat, as in chicken and fish, the quality most desired is freshness.

The cooking oil of choice is peanut oil; and if that is not available, then vegetable oil. Never use olive oil or butter. Flour is not used to thicken sauces but cornstarch.

American Chinese choose a wide variety of fresh vegetables. Although they do not eat raw green salads, they cook green vegetables carefully to retain color and crispness. Ordinarily they don't eat white potatoes, but yams or sweet potatoes.

Fresh noodles are sold in Chinatown, but dried egg-noodles may be used.

Milk and milk products have little place, although I have noticed that ice cream parlors are popular among the young in Chinatown as elsewhere; perhaps this is inspired by the deliciousness of ginger-flavored ice cream.

COOKING UTENSILS

No special utensils are really essential to prepare Chinese food; your own kitchen equipment is adequate. However, Oriental pots and pans make Chinese cooking more engaging, whether you want to try your hand at new Chinese dishes or entertain friends with delicious table-top novelties. Here is a list of the useful cooking utensils.

A wok is a round-bottomed cooking pan. It is marvelously efficient for stir-frying, the most common Chinese cooking method. An adaptor ring supports it above the heat-source. The 14 inch diameter wok is the most practical size.

An electric wok, as the name implies, is a traditional wok equipped with an electrical heating unit convenient for table-top cooking. It also gives controlled heat for stir-frying, deep frying; and, like any wok, becomes a steamer when covered with a lid.

A firepot, or Mongolian cooker, is a glorious brazen smokestack, ringed with a donut-shaped bowl shaped like a ring-mold. Broth simmers in the bowl, heated by charcoal in the base of the chimney. Guests seated around it do their own tabletop cooking in this communal pot, while the charcoal provides central heating for a cozy wintertime party.

A Genghis Khan grill is a crown-shaped iron for broiling meat. A small Genghis Khan household grill measures about 12 inches across and 2 inches high. It rests neatly over the burner of a stove, or over a bucket of sand and charcoal for outdoor cooking. Genghis Khan grills of giant size are used in restaurants here and the Far East.

A **steamer** in a Chinese kitchen does much of the work done by ovens in the West—therefore it is big: a 16-inch-diameter giant is practical for family cooking. The bottom of each tier of the steamer is a screen or lattice and many tiers can be piled up, under one lid, to cook everything at once. Most foods steamed in the steamer are in bowls or on platters. Put a damp cloth or paper towel under foods not in dishes.

A bamboo steamer is the traditional kind. It can rest directly in a wok. Use the steamer about once a week to keep it in condition.

Assembling A Steamer

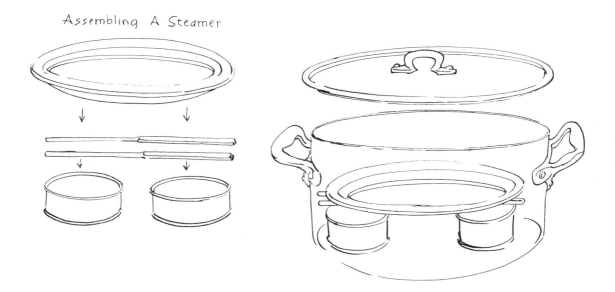

An improvised steamer can be made of a covered kettle. Steam must flow freely inside the kettle, so use a big kettle and a small bowl. To support the bowl, you can use foil pie pans with holes poked in them, one inverted and one right side up, or tuna cans with the ends removed. The bowl of food to be steamed must not touch the boiling water, and the water must be an inch deep.

Chinese Cleaver

The Chinese cleaver is so unlike a Western cleaver it deserves a different name altogether—just as Chinese wine, which is not wine, deserves its own name. In any case, we're stuck with "cleaver" which here means Chinese cleaver, a light-weight rectangular blade 3 1/2 inches deep and 8 inches long, with a wooden handle aligned to the top edge of the blade. The sharpened edge is slightly curved. It is manufactured in the United States as well as China.

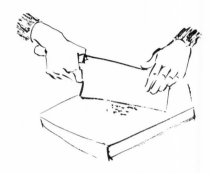

minces . . . (Hold the edge of the blade against the cutting board with your left hand)

It slices . . .

shreds into matchstick-size pieces . . . (Keep the fingers of your left hand curled under)

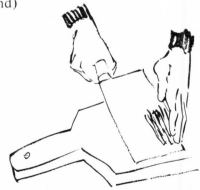

and it picks up the pieces from the cutting board . . . (Put down the blade like a dust pan and push them on to it)

crushes peppercorns . . . (Grind its handle in a bowl)

and it even opens a pouring hole in a can of chicken broth—if you're bold enough to strike a sharp blow.

The cleaver is as handy as chopsticks, and more easily mastered; but if you don't have one, you can work almost as well with a French Chef's knife or a Western cleaver.

Chopsticks

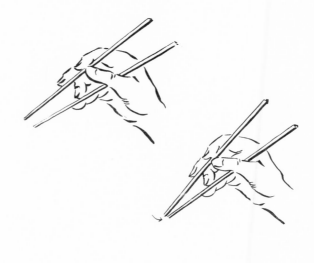

Chopsticks really aren't very difficult to use—besides, they make the food taste better.

The lower stick is stationary. The upper stick moves.

Small wire spoon used in Firepot dinners to scoop out ingredients simmering in the communal pot. Each guest has his own spoon.

STAPLES FOR THE CUPBOARD, REFRIGERATOR, AND FREEZER

A few basic staples on hand in the cupboard make last-minute cooking easier, and a change of plans possible. Besides tea, rice, flour, and canned chicken broth, keep these canned goods:

    bamboo shoots
    preserved turnip
    water chestnuts
. . . and these dried foods:
    bean threads
    chili peppers
    mushrooms
    noodles
    shrimp
. . . and this preserved food:
    preserved peppers

The following ingredients are used in many dishes. Keep them handy in the refrigerator:

    a quart or so of Basic Sauce
    several squares of bean cake. (Under water for a week's storage, or wrapped in paper towels for a few day's storage.)
. . . and in the vegetable compartment:
    Chinese cabbage
    fresh ginger root
    green onions

Many Chinese ingredients can be partially prepared and frozen ready for use. This is especially helpful in a Chinese meal where there are many dishes. It's always convenient to have a little savory pork stuffing in the freezer to put in a spring roll or little shelled shrimp ready to stir-fry with some fresh green vegetable or fine-sliced beef ready for the Genghis Khan Grill.

FREEZER

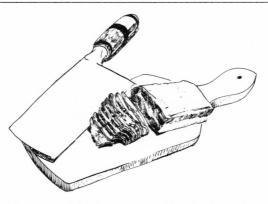

The freezer is especially useful if you remember that meat is easy to cut and trim before you put it in the freezer, and easy to slice fine after it is frozen. For instance, flank steak of beef: buy several at a time, cut them in half, trim away all the fat, and slice them lengthwise with the fiber about 2 inches wide. Wrap these sticks separately and freeze them. When it comes time to cook, the frozen stick may be sliced easily across the grain into 1/8 inch slices, and by the time the slices have marinated for ten minutes they will be thawed. The thinly sliced meat used in Chinese dishes thaws rapidly.

Fresh, boneless pork butt is another worthwhile meat to buy and freeze. Have half the pork ground by the butcher, and trim the other half into chunks about 1/2 inch thick, 2 inches wide, and as long as possible. Wrap them separately to freeze. Slice while still frozen, as above.

The ground pork should be mixed with marinade—about 4 Tbsp to 1/2 lb of pork, and 2 Tbsp cornstarch, and 1 Tbsp Chinese wine. Then pack it in covered plastic tubs to put in the freezer, in 4 oz (1/4 lb) lots. (Remember that a little goes a long way.) One of these small blocks out of the freezer can be cut into

1/2 inch slices to speed its thawing. Cut the block by pressing with both hands on the back of the cleaver.

Fresh shrimp or prawns can go into the freezer ready to use. Shell and split a pound of them; "wash" them with salt as explained in the stir-fry recipe for Shrimp Green. Rinse and dry the shrimp carefully, then stir in 3 Tbsp soy sauce and 1 Tbsp wine. Freeze in 4 oz lots in small plastic tubs. Thaw before cooking—it doesn't take long.

Fresh uncooked egg noodles may be stored in the freezer if you open the package first and separate them slightly. Some separation is required in storing won ton skins: divide them into stacks of four or so, and separate with wax paper before further wrapping.

Shredded ham, almonds, garnishes of many kinds can be frozen and ready for quick use. In fact, I find my freezer works for me better when it holds a lot of small plastic tubs than when it stores bulky bargains from the supermarket; the little tubs offer big choices in taste combinations, and short thawing, whereas that cutrate turkey tends to remain beyond its allotted time. Better let the supermarket store the turkey: they have more room.

The Chinese method of marinating meat and seafood for cooking is perfectly adapted for freezing. In addition to the soy sauce marinade, corn starch can be added to later absorb cooking juices, and ginger root to modulate the meat flavors. It's not only more convenient for the cook, but it also preserves the food.

THE ART OF MAKING CHINESE RICE

Two basic elements of Chinese cooking are rice and Basic Sauce.
Here are recipes for both:

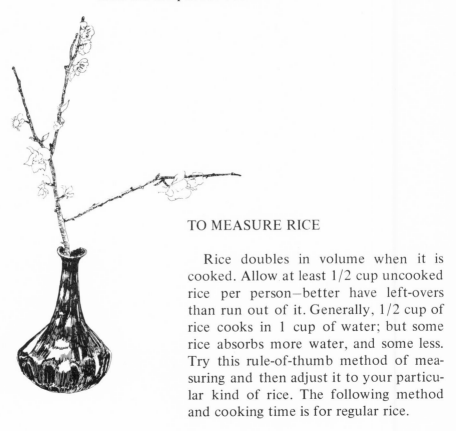

TO MEASURE RICE

Rice doubles in volume when it is cooked. Allow at least 1/2 cup uncooked rice per person—better have left-overs than run out of it. Generally, 1/2 cup of rice cooks in 1 cup of water; but some rice absorbs more water, and some less. Try this rule-of-thumb method of measuring and then adjust it to your particular kind of rice. The following method and cooking time is for regular rice.

TO WASH RICE

Measure the rice into a sturdy pot and set it under the cold kitchen tap. When the pot is full of water, stir the rice with your hand, and tip the pot so that most of the water runs out. Let the pot fill with water again, and stir and tip it again, 3 or 4 times, until the water is clear. Leave "one knuckle" of water above the top of the rice (about 3/4 inch). Let the rice sit in the water for about 1/2 hour before you start cooking it.

UNCOVERED POT METHOD

This method boils the rice but steams the kitchen. Use it if your stove has a blower-hood.

Set the pot over fairly high heat. When the water has boiled away and no more bubbles appear on the surface, turn the heat to low. The rice will make a low popping sound. Let it cook uncovered for about 20 minutes. Taste it now and then. If the pot is dry before the rice is done, add a little cold water.

COVERED POT METHOD

Bring rice to a boil over moderate heat. Cover, and cook at low heat until the water is gone. Poke a hole in the middle to see if the water is all absorbed into the rice; when it is, stir and fluff the rice, cover it again, and steam at very *low* heat for 20 minutes.

TO KEEP RICE HOT

At a buffet, where people are serving themselves at different times, and when cooked rice must be kept hot for late arrivals, keep the rice hot this way: Put it in a basket on a rack inside a big pot of water. Cover it, over very low heat. The basket may be an untreated bamboo washing basket or a colander lined with cheesecloth. A tuna can opened top and bottom makes a good rack; the water below should be an inch deep and not touch the basket; and the whole steamer can stay warm on a chafing dish or electric hot tray for several hours.

Soy Pot

BASIC SAUCE

Basic Sauce is a treasure in the Chinese kitchen, and it is simple to make. You can use it over and over again to slow-simmer any number of foods. It imparts its own rich flavor to what is cooked in it; and grows more savory the longer it lasts.

1 cup Dark soy sauce
1 cup Thin soy sauce
1 cup sugar
2 cups water
3 dried chili peppers
2 slices ginger root
2 Tbsp (5 whole flowerettes) star anise
1/2 cup peanut oil
2 cloves garlic, split

   Boil for 15 minutes

   Store sauce in the refrigerator. It keeps for months, and improves with time. As the sauce seasons, the balance of the flavors shifts. It becomes less salty as the salt is absorbed into foods; so add more soy sauce to compensate.

How to Use the Basic Sauce

Bring Basic Sauce to a full rolling boil, drop in the food to be cooked, turn off the heat immediately, and cover the pot. Set it in a warm place, like over a pilot light, or over a VERY low simmer burner. Be sure that your "simmer" is well below the boiling point, or it may toughen and dry out the meat.

Chicken gizzards: Simmer 25 minutes in Basic Sauce.

Chicken wings: Simmer 15 minutes in Basic Sauce.

Pork tripe: Parboil 15 minutes in water with a slice of ginger root. Drain, remove and discard the heavy white lining and fat; then slice it 1/2 inch wide. Simmer 15 minutes in Basic Sauce.

Pork ears: Parboil 15 minutes in water with slice of ginger root. Drain, slice 1/4 inch wide. Simmer 15 minutes in Basic Sauce.

Beef, chicken, pork liver, and heart: Simmer until done in Basic Sauce.

Tongue, large beef chunks, pork roasts: Simmer for the first half of the cooking time in water with a slice of ginger root and a green onion top; then in the Basic Sauce for the second half of the cooking time. For instance, simmer tongue 1 hour, remove, cool and peel. Then simmer 1 hour in Basic Sauce. If part of the meat is exposed remember to turn it over once during cooking. Use the cooking water for soup.

Bean cake: Put whole cake in Basic Sauce, bring to a boil, turn off the heat and set it aside for 10 minutes. Drain, and dry it in a warm oven for a few hours. Slice.

Eggs: Boil eggs in water 4 minutes, plunge into cold water, and shell them. Now simmer them for 40 minutes in the Basic Sauce. Drain, cool, and slice.

Fish: Simmer until done in Basic Sauce. Keep separate that portion of the Basic Sauce in which the fish was cooked, and use it only for cooking fish or for making a gravy for fish. Do not return it to the jar of Basic Sauce you will use for cooking other things.

Lamb: See instructions for fish, above.

Gravy for stir-fried or steamed dishes: Add 1/2 teaspoon cornstarch to 1/4 cup Basic Sauce. For stir-fried dishes, open up a space in the middle of the pan to pour in the gravy. Heat and stir until it is smooth and thickened. For steamed dishes, heat the gravy in a saucepan until it is smooth and thickened, then pour it over the food in the serving dish.

CHAPTER I

FIREPOT

When the weather is cold in the fall of the year, and we relish the cheering company of friends sitting around a warm and cozy table, it's time for a Peking Firepot Party!

We'll put our firepot in the middle of the dining table and pour in the hot broth. Into the broth we'll drop a variety of finely-sliced morsels of food—each of us choosing his own tidbits from a large platter of sliced meats, seafood, and vegetables. Each guest cooks his dinner to his own taste using a small wire spoon to net his tidbits. (In lieu of wire spoons, chopsticks can be used—but the results are more catch-as-catch can.)

Our party can be quite elaborate, with oysters and red-cooked pork. Or it can be simple, with chicken, bean curd, and lots of vegetables. While traditionally many ingredients go into a firepot dinner, you don't have to use them all, if you want to simplify the meal. Whatever the case, the mood is festive!

Our firepot can be a real Chinese firepot, big, brass, and chimneyed; or it can be any big pot that fits over a hot plate; or even a large chafing dish. An electric wok also doubles for a firepot. Actually, all you need is a good sized pot that can be placed in the center of the table and kept sufficiently hot to simmer broth.

The size of a firepot party is limited to the number of guests who can reach the pot while seated at the table; no more than six. (Of course, you could set up a second table, with another firepot, for six more.)

If you use a Chinese firepot, remember these basic rules: Heat in the firepot comes from radiant charcoal on a grate above the base of the chimney. You should light the charcoal and burn it in a heavy iron frying pan in a broiler, or in an outside barbecue grill; and then put the glowing coals into the firepot. Some firepots come apart for this stoking-up, while others must be loaded from the top of the chimney with tongs. The moat-shaped bowl that holds the broth must have a little hot water in it when you put in the coals.

Be ready for a lot of heat when the coals warm up the brass chimney. The firepot should be put firmly in place in the middle of a good-sized table, on top of an insulator—an asbestos pad or a pan of water.

Heat the broth or soup on the stove, and transfer it to the firepot bowl, when you're ready to dine. Ingredients must be ready, too, and arranged on platters around the firepot.

Set the table with a plate, a bowl, and chopsticks, before each place. A wire spoon may also be provided for each guest.

The following standard condiments should be placed on the table:

hot oil
rice vinegar
sesame oil
mustard sauce (Mix dry mustard into a paste with vinegar)
Hoisin sauce, if available (Bottled, sold in Chinese markets)

PEKING FIREPOT

2 lbs tenderloin of lamb, sliced very thin
1/4 cup soy sauce
2 tsp cornstarch
2 cups boiling water
6 oz bean threads
1 large chunk preserved turnip, minced
1 lb Chinese cabbage, quartered and sliced
1/2 lb noodles, cooked and drained

Marinate lamb in soy sauce mixed with cornstarch.

Pour boiling water over bean threads and soak them for 1/2 hour. Drain.

Assemble the firepot with hot charcoal, and fill the bowl half full with boiling water. Add preserved turnip, Chinese cabbage and noodles.

Each guest now mixes a sauce to his own taste in his own bowl, out of the following ingredients on the table. The liquids can be put in cruets and the sesame seeds and green onions in bowls. Allow 1 cup for each ingredient.

> soy sauce
> rice vinegar
> Chinese wine (Kao Liang)
> hot oil
> sesame seeds, roasted and ground
> green onion, chopped

When the water simmers in the pot again, each guest picks up a piece of lamb and holds it in the broth for the quarter-minute it takes to cook, then dips it in his bowl of sauce.

When the meal is nearly over, add the bean threads to the firepot. Ladle out the remaining soup and bean threads into every one's bowl so your guests may savor the soup last.

WINTER HOTPOT

Don't be dismayed by the number of ingredients in any of these Firepot recipes. As we said in the introduction, the number of ingredients you want to use is up to you, and so are any substitutions you care to make. A Firepot dinner is taster's choice!

1/2 fresh chicken (about 3 or 4 lbs)
1 lb pork tenderloin

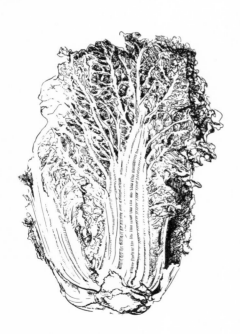

5 cups water
1/2 cup soy sauce
1 tsp salt
3 bean cakes
4 oz bean threads
2 cups boiling water
1 egg white, beaten
1 tsp Chinese wine
1 tsp cornstarch
1/4 lb fresh shrimp, peeled and deveined
1/4 lb fresh white fish fillets, cut in
   1 inch squares
1/2 pint fresh oysters
1 tsp soy sauce
1/2 tsp cornstarch
1/2 lb Chinese cabbage, quartered &
   sliced 1/2 inch wide
1/4 lb good quality ham, or Italian
   proscuitto, sliced
1/4 lb bamboo shoots, sliced
2 stalks minced green onions

Simmer chicken and pork in water combined with soy sauce and salt for 1 1/2 hours. Drain and save the broth. Chop chicken into bite-sized pieces; the pork into 1 inch cubes.

Cut bean cake into 4 cubes and deep fry until brown. (The fried bean cake and chicken and pork can be prepared the day before, if you like.)

Cover bean threads with boiling water, and soak for 1/2 hour. Drain.

Mix together egg white, wine, and cornstarch and marinate shrimp and fish fillets.

Marinate oysters in soy sauce and cornstarch.

Arrange all ingredients neatly on platters and bring to the table.

Assemble the firepot with glowing charcoal inside. Heat the broth obtained from cooking the chicken and pork, and pour it into the bowl of the firepot. Add sufficient boiling water so the firepot is half full.

When the broth starts to simmer, put the ingredients into the firepot in the following order: cabbage, bean cake, chicken, pork, bean threads, oysters, ham, bamboo shoots, shrimp, fish fillets, and green onions. (Guests may help with this project if they like.) Cover firepot.

When the firepot simmers again, each guest helps himself to the pot. For this meal there should be a bowl of rice at every place.

CHIMNEY SOUP

In this version of the firepot dinner, each guest makes his own choice of ingredients and cooks them in the simmering pot using chopsticks or a wire spoon.

Meat:	1 lb flank steak, sliced fine (easy to slice if frozen)	Chicken:	1 breast of chicken, boned, sliced thin
Marinade:	1/4 cup soy sauce		1/2 lb chicken liver in thin slices
	1 Tbsp cornstarch		
	1 Tbsp Chinese wine or ginger juice	Seafood:	1/2 lb shrimp, shelled and deveined, cut in half

1 lb fillets of fish, cut in
  1 inch squares
2 cups chicken broth
Salt to taste
Vegetables: 1 Chinese cabbage, quartered
  and sliced 1/2 inch wide
  Cauliflower or broccoli
    flowerettes, sliced 1/4
    inch thick
  3 stalks green onions, sliced
  1/2 lb fresh mushrooms,
    sliced
  1 bunch spinach, washed and
    broken into large pieces
  1 turnip, sliced in match-
    stick strips
  1 bunch Chinese parsley,
    minced for garnish
    (don't put in broth)
  4 squares bean cake, each
    cut in 9 cubes
  2 oz bean threads. Pour 1
    cup boiling water over
    them, soak for 1/2 hour,
    drain.
1/2 lb noodles, cooked and drained

You can offer your guests a selection of as many of the above ingredients as you like. The wider the variety, the more interesting the meal.

Mix the Marinade and pour it over the meat, chicken, and seafood.

Assemble the firepot with glowing charcoal. Half fill the bowl with boiling water, and add chicken broth. Salt to taste. (Add more boiling water to the bowl if it gets low during the dinner.) Arrange all ingredients on platters; bring them to the table and let guests help themselves.

At the end of the meal, stir cooked noodles into remaining broth which is then served as a soup.

Traditionally, each guest is provided a small raw egg to break into his bowl before ladling in the hot soup. The egg then cooks in the broth.

CHRYSANTHEMUM BOWL

This gala-occasion treat is best made in a large chafing dish, or electric wok. Guests help with the cooking, and the fun is shared by all.

2 Tbsp Chinese wine
1 Tbsp cornstarch
2 Tbsp water
1/2 lb pork in 1/8 inch slices
1 chicken breast, boned, skinned and
   sliced fine
1/2 lb shrimp, shelled and deveined,
   sliced lengthwise
1/2 lb chicken, duck, or pork liver,
   sliced fine
2 pork kidneys, outer 1/4 inch only,
   sliced fine (optional)
1/4 lb small fresh oysters, shucked
Chicken broth and water in equal
   amounts to half-fill bowl
Salt to taste
2 2 oz packages bean threads, deep fried
   1/2 minute at 390 degrees
1/2 lb Chinese cabbage, shredded
1/4 lb spinach leaves, washed and broken
   into large pieces
1 large white chrysanthemum flower,
   petals only, washed

Mix together wine, cornstarch and water and spoon a little over each bowl of meat, chicken and seafood.

Heat chicken broth and water and pour it into chafing dish. Salt to taste. Bring the platters of food to the table. When the pot simmers again, everyone helps put half the ingredients into the pot (with the exception of the chrysanthemum petals).

When the pot has simmered for 5 minutes, the food is cooked and guests help themselves to the succulent feast. As the ingredients are consumed, the pot is replenished.

Finally, when there is only broth left in the pot, it is time to put in the petals of chrysanthemum flower. These delicately flavor the broth that is then served as an after-dinner soup.

Chrysanthemums

CHAPTER II

TABLE-TOP STIR-FRY

Table-top stir-fry cooking can be done wherever you get sufficient heat in a cooking pan—on a dining table, sideboard, or outside picnic table. An electric wok works very well for this; so does an electric frying pan, or a wok over a brazier. For a new and original way of entertaining, plan a small party around the cooking pan—and bring your kitchen to the table.

Stir-frying is a marvelous Chinese way of cooking that conserves the freshness, lightness, and succulence of food. This is done by:

1. Proper cutting: pieces are uniform in size so they are all done at the same time.

2. Short cooking time, so nothing has time to toughen or grow soggy.

3. High heat and rapid stirring, so every piece is lightly seared on all sides during its short stay in the wok.

A Chinese wok is generally used for stir-frying because its shape concentrates the action into a small central area of the pan, for perfect control by the chef. (However, Chinese cooking is a method, not a device, and you can stir-fry foods very well on the stove in your old iron skillet.)

Because stir-frying is done so rapidly, all ingredients must be ready—there is no time for preparation after stir-frying has begun. Therefore, the sliced and shredded raw foods are piled on a platter, beforehand, and set beside the wok along with the seasonings. Here is where guests can help you, if they like, with the chopping and slicing of the many ingredients which will then be cooked in the stir-fry.

Each dish in the following section can be a main course, but should be served with several other dishes in the Chinese manner. I recommend combining one or two table-top stir-fry recipes with one or two dishes that can be prepared in the kitchen in the steamer, oven, or simmering pot. (See Chapter V, Peking Kitchen).

SPICED BEEF

Have all your ingredients ready in bowls, and cook each ingredient in succession in the same wok. Finally, all ingredients are combined in the wok and stir-fried.

1 lb flank steak, sliced 1/8 inch thick
   across the grain
Marinade: 3 Tbsp soy sauce
             2 tsp cornstarch
             2 Tbsp peanut oil
             1/2 clove garlic, minced
Sauce: 2 tsp ginger root, minced
             2 Tbsp soy sauce
             2 Tbsp vinegar
             2 tsp sugar
             2 tsp preserved pepper,
                chopped
Thickener: 1 tsp cornstarch
             1/2 cup water or chicken
                broth
2 Tbsp peanut oil
1/2 cup bamboo shoots, sliced in matchstick strips
1/2 cup celery, sliced in matchstick strips
1/2 cup yellow onion, sliced in matchstick strips

Stir steak slices in Marinade. Mix together the ingredients for Sauce. Mix together the cornstarch and water for the Thickener.

Heat a wok, add 1 Tbsp peanut oil. Add bamboo shoots, celery, and onion. Stir-fry for 2 minutes and remove them from the wok.

Add 1 Tbsp more of peanut oil to the hot wok, and put in the steak slices. Stir-fry only until they are half done: about 1/2 minute. Remove them from the wok.

Now heat Sauce in the wok, and add about half of the Thickener. Stir until it is smooth and slightly thick, adding more Thickener if it is needed. Add the vegetables. When they are hot, turn off the heat and add the beef and the beef juice that has exuded from it. Stir, and serve immediately.

SHRIMP GREEN

1 lb fresh shrimp, shelled and deveined
2 Tbsp salt
Marinade: 1 tsp cornstarch
             1 tsp ginger juice
             1 tsp green onions, minced
             1/2 tsp salt
             2 tsp soy sauce
             1 tsp wine
2 cups shelled green peas
1 yellow onion, diced
6 Tbsp peanut oil
Salt to taste

"Butterfly" each shrimp by slicing about 1/4 inch deep into its back, lengthwise. This makes it curl and look bulkier when it is heated.

"Wash" the shrimp to firm them up: stir together with 2 Tbsp salt, and press them hard with your hands against the inside of a colander to squeeze out as much juice as possible. Rinse under running water and dry with a towel.

Stir Marinade into shrimp and set in refrigerator for 15 minutes.

Boil peas until barely done, and drain.

Heat wok and saute onion in 1 Tbsp peanut oil; remove from wok.

Reheat the wok, add 5 Tbsp peanut oil. Add the shrimp and stir-fry for 1 minute. Add the peas and onions, salt to taste. Stir once, and remove to a serving dish.

FRIED CHICKEN WITH GREEN PEPPER

1 whole chicken breast, boned
Marinade: 2 Tbsp soy sauce
              2 tsp cornstarch
              3 slices ginger root
              3 stalks green onion, minced
              1/2 egg white, beaten
              1/2 tsp salt
              1 Tbsp Chinese wine
2 Tbsp peanut oil
1 yellow onion, diced 1/2 inch cubes
2 green peppers, diced 3/4 inch squares
1/4 cup chicken broth, or water
2 dried chili peppers, broken in pieces
1 clove garlic, minced
Salt to taste
1/2 cup shelled roasted peanuts

Dice the chicken into 1/2 inch cubes, removing the tendons as you work. Cut the skin into 1/2 inch squares. Mix the Marinade, pour it over the chicken, and set aside for 15 minutes.

Heat a wok, add 1 Tbsp peanut oil, and stir-fry the onion cubes for 4 minutes. Then add green peppers & chicken broth or water, cover, and steam until cooked. Remove from wok.

Heat the wok and add 1 more Tbsp of peanut oil. Add the pieces of dried chili and stir until they are brown (your eyes may smart a bit, but the flavor is worth it!) Add the garlic and chicken. Stir-fry until done.

Add green pepper and onion, stirring, to rewarm them. Salt to taste. Serve this dish garnished with the peanuts.

HOT BEAN CAKE

1/4 lb ground beef
Marinade: 2 tsp soy sauce
                 1/2 tsp salt
                 1 tsp cornstarch
                 1 tsp ginger juice
                 1 tsp hot oil
2 Tbsp peanut oil
2 Tbsp green onion, minced
3 Tbsp water chestnuts, sliced

1 egg-sized chunk preserved turnip,
    minced
4 to 6 squares of bean cake, cut in
    1/4 inch cubes*
1 cup chicken broth
Thickener: 1 tsp cornstarch
                  3 Tbsp water
1/2 tsp Szechwan pepper

Mix ground beef with Marinade and set it aside for 10 minutes.

Heat a wok, add 1 Tbsp peanut oil, and stir-fry the ground beef for 1/2 minute. Remove from pan.

Reheat the wok, and add 1 Tbsp peanut oil, green onion, water chestnuts, turnip, and bean cake. Stir them together, add chicken broth and the ground beef; cover and simmer for 15 minutes.

Pour the Thickener into the middle of the pan, and stir until the sauce is smooth and slightly thickened. Pour it into a serving dish and sprinkle Szechwan pepper over it.

*If the bean cake is too soft to cut easily, put it into the wok whole, and mash it with a fork.

PORK LIVER

Rich liver, bland vegetables, with more than a touch of heat.

1-1/2 lb pork liver
Marinade: 2 Tbsp soy sauce
                    2 tsp cornstarch
                    2 tsp ginger juice
2 Tbsp peanut oil
1 yellow onion, cut lengthwise into
    1/4 inch strips
2 stalks celery, sliced diagonally 1/8
    inch strips
1 bamboo shoot, cut into matchstick
    strips
1 tsp ginger root, minced
1/4 tsp Szechwan pepper
1 tsp hot oil
2 green onions, cut lengthwise into
    matchstick strips
2 preserved peppers, minced
Salt to taste
Garnish: chives and Chinese parsley

Trim pork liver of all connective tissue. Cut into strips 1/4 inch square and 2 inches long. Mix with Marinade.

Heat 1 Tbsp peanut oil in wok, add onion, then celery and bamboo; stir-fry for 1 minute, and remove from wok.

Add 1 Tbsp peanut oil to the hot pan, and fry ginger strips 1/4 minute. Add pork liver and stir-fry 1 minute; then add Szechwan pepper, hot oil, green onion, and preserved peppers. Then add the celery and bamboo shoots for another 1/4 minute. Salt to taste. Remove immediately to a serving dish.

Garnish with chives and Chinese parsley.

CHICKEN GIZZARDS & PEAS

1 lb chicken gizzards
Marinade: 1 Tbsp soy sauce
             2 tsp cornstarch
             1 tsp ginger juice
1 Tbsp peanut oil

1 slice ginger
1 pkg. frozen peas, or 1 cup fresh peas,
   parboiled 3 minutes
1/4 cup water chestnuts, sliced
Salt to taste

Remove the skin of the gizzards: pull it away with your fingers, if possible, after making an initial knife-cut; or, slice it away with a sharp knife.

Slice each gizzard 1/4 inch thick, then score it with several slashes in a criss-cross pattern on one side. This is for a party dish. For family style, slice the gizzards 1/8 inch thick.

Mix gizzards with Marinade, and set them aside for 20 minutes.

Heat wok, add 1 Tbsp peanut oil, and then the slice of ginger. Add the chicken gizzards, stir-fry for 3 minutes, or until they are done. Add the peas and water chestnuts. Salt to taste. Stir-fry together for 1/4 minute to warm them, and serve immediately.

PORK WITH BEAN CAKE

1/2 lb pork, cut into 1/2 inch cubes
Marinade: 2 Tbsp soy sauce
             2 tsp starch
2 Tbsp peanut oil
4 bean cakes, cut into 3/8 inch cubes
2 green onions, cut in matchstick strips
2 Tbsp Black Bean Sauce,* stirred with
   1 Tbsp water
1 tsp hot oil
1/2 lb shelled roasted peanuts
Salt to taste

Mix the pork cubes with Marinade and set aside for 10 minutes.

Heat a wok, add 1 Tbsp peanut oil, and stir-fry the bean cake cubes at medium heat for 1 minute. Remove from pan. Put the green onion in the pan, stir-fry it quickly and remove.

Reheat the wok and add 1 Tbsp peanut oil. Add the pork cubes, and stir-fry for 2 minutes. Add the Black Bean Sauce and hot oil, and stir and cook for 2 more minutes. Add the green onion, bean cake, and peanuts, stir, salt to taste, and serve at once.

*See page 9

CLOUDS' EARS, SNOW PEAS, AND CHICKEN

Clouds' ears are tree mushrooms with a flavor as delicate as their name. They are valued for their crisp consistency. They require soaking but almost no cooking.

1 chicken breast, boned, tendons
   removed, and cut in 1/2 inch cubes
Marinade: 1 egg white, lightly beaten
           1 tsp ginger juice
           1/2 tsp salt
4 Tbsp peanut oil
1 cup snow peas, fresh or frozen and
   thawed
1 green onion, minced
1/4 cup chicken broth or water
1 slice ginger root
1 cup dried clouds' ears, soaked and
   sliced 1/4 inch wide
Salt to taste
1/4 tsp Szechwan pepper

Mix the Marinade and the chicken cubes together; and set aside for 20 minutes.

Heat a wok, add 1 Tbsp peanut oil, and stir-fry the snow peas and green onion for 1 minute. Turn the heat down to low, add the chicken broth or water, and cover and steam for 1 minute. Remove from wok.

Reheat the wok, and add 3 Tbsp peanut oil. Add the slice of ginger root; add and stir-fry the chicken pieces for 1 minute. Add the clouds' ears and stir-fry for 1 minute. Add the snow peas. Salt to taste. Stir briefly, and remove to a serving plate. Sprinkle Szechwan pepper over it.

PORK, TURNIP & BEAN STRIPS

1/2 lb pork, cut in 1/8 inch strips,
   1/4 inch wide
Marinade: 2 Tbsp soy sauce
              2 tsp cornstarch
              1 tsp ginger juice
4 bean cakes, cut in strips as thin as
   possible, 1/4 inch wide
4 Tbsp peanut oil

2 red bell peppers, in strips 1/4 inch
   wide
    or
1/4 lb snow peas (pea pods), sliced
   lengthwise 1/4 inch wide
1/2 cup preserved turnip, in matchstick
   strips
Salt to taste

Mix together the pork strips and Marinade.

Heat a wok, add 1 Tbsp peanut oil, gently lay the bean cake strips over the bottom of the pan, and saute for 4 minutes each side, lifting and turning the strips over once. Heat must be at Low-Medium, and bean cake strips must be watched carefully so they don't burn. Remove from wok.

Reheat the wok, add 1 Tbsp peanut oil, and stir-fry the peppers for 1 minute. Remove from wok.

Reheat the wok, add 2 Tbsp peanut oil, and stir-fry the pork strips for 3 minutes. Add the preserved turnip and stir-fry together for 1 minute. Add the peppers and bean cake strips, stir several times to reheat evenly, salt to taste, and serve.

SHRIMP MUSHROOMS

1 lb medium-sized fresh shrimp, peeled
   and deveined
Marinade: 1 egg white, lightly beaten
            1 tsp sesame oil
            1 tsp salt
            1 Tbsp wine
            2 tsp cornstarch

3 Tbsp peanut oil
1 tsp ginger root, sliced in fine strips
1/2 cup green onion, in matchstick strips
1/4 cup water chestnuts, sliced 1/8 inch
   thick
1/2 cup fresh peas, or 1/2 pkg. frozen
   peas; parboiled 3 minutes and drained
1/2 cup canned button mushrooms

Butterfly and "wash" the shrimp. (See p. 50.)

Mix them with Marinade and set in refrigerator for 20 minutes.

Heat a wok, add 2 Tbsp peanut oil and ginger strips. Add shrimp, and stir-fry for 1 minute. Remove the shrimp.

Reheat the wok, add 1 Tbsp peanut oil, and add green onion, water chestnuts, peas, and mushrooms. Add the shrimp, stir several times to reheat, salt to taste, and serve immediately.

PORK & TURNIP

1/2 lb pork, cut in thin strips 1/4 inch
   wide
Marinade: 2 Tbsp soy sauce
            1 Tbsp cornstarch
            1 tsp sugar
2 Tbsp peanut oil
1 yellow onion, cut lengthwise into
   matchstick strips
2 green peppers, cut into matchstick
   strips

          or

5 stalks asparagus, cut diagonally into
   1/8 inch slices

          or

1/4 lb snow peas (pea pods), sliced
   lengthwise 1/4 inch wide
1/4 cup preserved turnip, cut into
   matchstick strips
1/4 cup bamboo shoots, cut in 1/4 inch
   strips
Salt to taste

Mix the pork strips with Marinade and set aside for 15 minutes.

Heat wok, add 1 Tbsp peanut oil, and stir-fry the yellow onion until done (about 2 minutes). Remove from wok. Add 1 Tbsp peanut oil, and stir-fry the green pepper, or asparagus or snow peas, until barely done (about 3 minutes). Remove from wok.

Reheat the wok, and add 1 Tbsp peanut oil. Add the pork with preserved turnip and bamboo shoot, and stir-fry for 2 minutes. Add the peppers and onions, stir several times, salt to taste, and serve.

CHAPTER III

CHINESE BARBECUES

Any nice day is the time for a picnic, Chinese style. One of the tastiest picnic feasts, traditionally cooked on a Genghis Khan grill, is Mongolian Lamb.

Mongolian Lamb is an imaginative dish for a small outdoor party. Everyone grills his own meat on the charcoal brazier placed in the middle of the table. Holding a bowl in one hand and chopsticks in the other, each guest picks up a piece of thinly sliced, marinated lamb from a communal platter and then places it briefly on the grill. After a few seconds, the meat is turned over and then put in the bowl before being eaten. (Chopsticks are quickly mastered when inspired by an outdoor appetite.)

Plain yeast rolls of flour tortilla pancakes (convenient substitutes for the traditional steamed bread or Mandarin pancakes) may be served for those who like to eat their lamb like a sandwich—or wrapped in a pancake. (Warm the flour tortillas in a steamer for twenty minutes.)

The crown-shaped Genghis Khan grill is ideal for this barbecue since the grooved surface securely holds the thinly sliced meat. However, you may use any table grill you like—as long as it's covered with a wire mesh. Hibachis are also practical for table top barbecues.

Light the charcoal briquets about 40 minutes before cooking time. When they are glowing and covered with ash, put them on a bed of sand in the fire box under your grill.

MONGOLIAN LAMB

2 lbs boneless lamb, sliced thin
Marinade: 1/4 cup soy sauce
            1 Tbsp wine or 1 tsp garlic
               juice
            1 Tbsp Hoisin sauce*
            1 tsp salt
            3 cloves garlic, minced
            1 bunch green onions,
               chopped

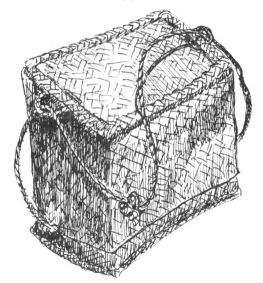

Chinese Lunch Box

The lamb is easiest to slice when it is frozen. Lay the slices one layer deep on plastic wrap, brush them with Marinade, and wrap them up carefully. Marinade permeates the lamb as it thaws, and if you unwrap it carefully it remains neatly arranged. After you have unwrapped it, spoon the rest of the Marinade over the lamb. This is an easy way to prepare it for a picnic.

Marinate the lamb for 1 hour or longer before bringing it to the table.

Mongolian Lamb may also be pan fried over high heat.

*Available in Oriental markets.

GARLIC JUICE

A half-teaspoonful of garlic juice is frequently added as a flavoring in cooking lamb. It's also used to flavor many marinades and sauces. Here is a convenient way to put the fresh essence of garlic into a bottle.

1/4 cup garlic cloves, peeled
1/2 cup soy sauce
1 Tbsp wine

Spin garlic and soy sauce together in a blender, and pour it into a small, covered jar. Pour the wine over it. Refrigerate.

Soy Pot

HONEY HAM

1 lb Virginia ham*
1 cup rock sugar
Thickener: 1 tsp cornstarch
1/2 cup water

Trim skin and fat from ham. Simmer 20 minutes, drain. Slice ham thinly, put it in a bowl, sprinkle 1/2 cup rock sugar over it, and steam it for 20 minutes according to instructions on page 23 .

To make a sauce: Drain meat juice left in the bowl after steaming into a saucepan. Warm juices with the remaining 1/2 cup sugar, and thicken with cornstarch and water.

Dip each ham slice into sugar sauce and grill until it is brown on the edges.

*If cooked ham is substituted here, it does not need to be boiled.

CHICKEN LEGS

In the Chinese kitchen, each part of the chicken has a special use. For example, the chicken thigh is boned and used like breast in Chicken Salad or Chicken and Green Pepper. The drumsticks, which tend to be left over, have their own recipe. Here it is.

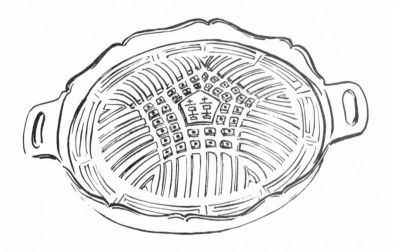

8 or 10 chicken legs
Marinade: **1/4 cup soy sauce**
            1 tsp ginger juice

Marinate the legs for 1 hour or more.

Heat the Genghis Khan grill, and prop the legs on it with their bony ends in the trough. Grill for 50 minutes, turning occasionally; and basting with the remaining Marinade.

CHINESE MIXED GRILL

Barbecue these meats & vegetables on skewers over a standard grill.

Choose a combination of several meats and vegetables. Cut things for each skewer into uniformly-sized chunks. Meat may be sliced fine, then folded and skewered.

Boneless pork, beef, or lamb; in slices or small meatballs
Chicken, boned, or chicken wings
Large shrimp, combined with chicken livers
Onions, scallions, green pepper, asparagus, mushrooms, eggplant
Marinade: 1/2 cup soy suace
             1/4 cup lemon juice and
               1 Tbsp sugar
                or
             1/2 cup pineapple juice
             1 tsp garlic juice
             1 tsp ginger juice

Marinate pork for 48 hours in refrigerator. Other meat for 24 hours.

Bamboo skewers should be soaked in water for several hours so they resist burning.

Thread ingredients on skewers and grill over charcoal until cooked.

CHAPTER IV

MANDARIN PANCAKE PARTIES

Mandarin pancakes, served with a choice of savory fillings, can be an original lunch, or supper, for a small and informal party. Everyone fills his own pancakes; first spooning on a little sauce, and then adding a few morsels from one or another of the serving dishes. The pancake, which is eaten like a sandwich, is rolled up, with one end turned in like the cover of a package. (To keep pancakes hot and moist during the meal, wrap them in a warm, damp napkin.)

If the word pancake suggests a flannel cake to you—doughy in the mouth and leaden in the stomach—be assured these are pancakes with a difference! Mandarin pancakes are invitingly delicate since they're artfully rolled out paper-thin.

MANDARIN PANCAKES

1-1/2 cups flour
1/2 cup hot water
2 Tbsp vegetable oil in a saucer

Mix flour and water to form a rather stiff dough. Knead it for 10 minutes, then cover it and let it rest for 20 minutes.

Roll the dough out with a rolling pin to make a sheet; then roll it up with your hands to make a solid stick. Cut this stick of dough into walnut-sized chunks. Cover them while you are rolling out the pancakes.

Flatten a walnut-sized chunk of dough to about dollar size. Spread oil on one side of it, using the back of a spoon.

Press another dollar sized piece of dough to the oiled side and roll the pair of them out thin, 6 or 7 inches in diameter, turning frequently on the board.

Roll out several pancakes and then "bake" them in a hot, lightly oiled frying pan set over a very low heat so the pancakes bake rather than fry. Turn them once. They should have air-bubbles and be slightly browned. Separate the two halves of the pancake as soon as you remove it from the pan. If the separation is not easy, it's because part of the surface did not get oiled.

Stack the baked pancakes in a covered dish as you work. Like the dough, they must be covered at all times, so they don't dry out.

Make the pancakes beforehand, if you prefer. Refrigerate them for a few days, or freeze them. Put a layer of muslin, or wax paper, between every three or four pancakes; and wrap them snugly before you refrigerate or freeze them.

To warm them again, after they have been frozen or refrigerated or simply cooled off: wrap in a dampened tea towel and put them on a rack in a steamer. (See Improvised Steamer, p. 23) Then remove a few at a time as they are served.

On the table, besides the pancakes and the following serving dishes of fillings, there should be bowls, or cruets, of:

hot mustard sauce	watercress, chopped
hot oil	green onion, minced
sesame oil	Chinese parsley
Hoisin sauce	

Another traditional accompaniment to a Mandarin Pancake party are marinated green onions. Use about 4 or 5 inches of the white end of green onions. Split the onion lengthwise. Then make 4 cuts at each end, 1 inch long, toward the center. Immerse onions completely in white vinegar overnight or longer. Drain, and chill.

FILLING: BEAN SPROUTS, GREEN PEPPER & PORK

1/2 lb pork, sliced very thin
Marinade: 1 Tbsp soy sauce
              1 tsp salt
              1 tsp cornstarch
              1 tsp ginger juice
2 Tbsp peanut oil
2 green peppers, sliced in matchstick
    pieces
1 lb bean sprouts

Marinate the pork slices.

Heat a wok, add peanut oil, and stir-fry the pork slices for a minute.

Add the green peppers and stir-fry for 3 minutes.

Add the bean sprouts and stir-fry for 2 minutes. Salt to taste, and serve.

FILLING: BARBECUED PORK

1 lb pork tenderloin, in chunks about an
   inch square and 4 inches long
Marinade: 1 tsp ginger root, minced
           4 green onions, 2 inches
              from the white ends
              only, split lengthwise
           1/2 tsp hot oil
           3/4 cup soy sauce
           2 Tbsp sugar

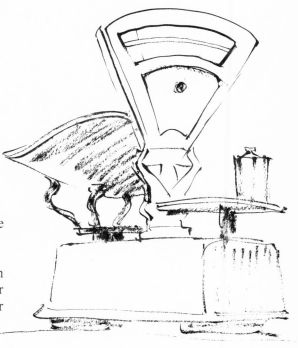

Mix pork and Marinade. Refrigerate
for 4 hours or more.

Set oven to 325. Lay pork in a pan
3-1/2 inches under the broiler flame for
25 minutes; turn over and bake the other
side for 20 minutes.

To serve, cut each piece diagonally
into slices about 3/8 inch thick. Rear-
range on a platter.

FILLING: SCRAMBLED EGGS WITH CHICKEN

1/2 lb chicken breasts and thighs, boned,
  in thin slices
Marinade: 1 Tbsp soy sauce
            1 tsp ginger juice
            1 tsp cornstarch
6 Tbsp peanut oil
3 eggs, lightly beaten, with a dash of salt
1/2 stalk green onion, sliced
1 slice ginger root, minced
1 chunk bamboo shoot, shredded
2 dried mushrooms, soaked and sliced
6 clouds' ears, soaked
1 Tbsp ginger juice
1/2 tsp salt
1-1/2 Tbsp soy sauce

Marinate the chicken slices.

Heat a wok, add 2 Tbsp of the peanut oil, and quickly scramble the eggs. Remove them from the wok.

Reheat the wok and add 2 Tbsp peanut oil. Stir-fry the chicken slices until they are done—about 6 minutes. Remove them from the wok.

Reheat the wok and add remaining 2 Tbsp peanut oil. Add and stir-fry: green onion, ginger, bamboo shoot, mushrooms, clouds' ears.

Add the ginger juice, salt, and soy sauce. Add the scrambled eggs and chicken, and mix quickly. Serve immediately.

CHAPTER V

THE PEKING KITCHEN

How do you manage to cook a real Chinese dinner with a different dish for each person, and yet have all the dishes ready to be served at the same time? The answer is, while you're stir-frying one dish at the table, the others are simmering on the stove or roasting in the oven.

The Chinese kitchen produces a remarkable variety of succulent dishes cooked in a steamer, pot, oven, or deep fat fryer. All these cooking methods are familiar to Westerners, but in some instances the methods vary. Some meat is fried twice, as in Sweet and Sour Pork; and the process of wet-steaming is used more frequently in Oriental cooking. In Chinese kitchens, a big steam kettle with many tiers can cook breads, dumplings, sweet rice, and meat all at once. In our American kitchens, a small steamer is easily improvised (p. 23) that can cook food as savory —but one dish at a time.

For a beginning, try your hand at Tea Eggs, Steamed Chicken, or Pork Shoulder Roast. Then sample the Rock Cod, or the Fried Fish Fillets. One of the most popular dishes in the Peking kitchen is the Mandarin Fried Rice which has room for any tasty leftovers.

PORK IN GREEN PEPPER CUPS

This tasty dish may be easily cooked in a Western kitchen using a flat-bottomed cooking pan. Substitutions for Chinese specialty items are suggested below.

Stuffing Mix:
- 1/2 lb ground pork
- 2 Tbsp soy sauce
- 2 tsp cornstarch
- 1 tsp sesame oil (or 1 tsp peanut oil)
- 1 egg
- 1/2 cup water chestnuts, minced (or 1/2 cup celery, finely cut)
- 1 Tbsp green onion, minced
- 1 tsp salt
- 1/2 tsp black pepper

5 medium-sized green peppers, halved lengthwise, seeds removed
3 Tbsp peanut oil

Gravy:
- 1 cup chicken stock
- 4 Tbsp soy sauce
- 1 Tbsp sugar

Mix the Stuffing Mix ingredients in the order in which they are given. Press the Stuffing Mix into green pepper halves.

Heat a flat-bottomed pan, add peanut oil, and pan fry the stuffed pepper cups on both sides until brown.

Mix together the ingredients for the gravy and add to the cooking pan. Simmer covered for 10 minutes. Salt to taste.

STEAMED CHICKEN

1 Fresh chicken, cut (straight through the bones, Chinese style) into rather large bite-sized pieces. Reserve the breast, as white meat tends to get tough with steaming, and use it for a stir-fried dish.

Marinade: 4 Tbsp soy sauce
               2 tsp cornstarch
               2 tsp salt

2 tsp sesame oil
4 fried mushrooms, soaked, sliced 1/4 inch wide
1/2 cup fresh pork, in very fine matchstick strips

Marinate chicken 10 minutes. Add the sesame oil, mushrooms, and pork strips, and set it aside for 20 minutes.

Arrange the chicken pieces in a glass platter or shallow porcelain bowl. All the top meat must be covered with skin.

Steam for 20–30 minutes.

SPICED FISH

A whole fish may be fried in a wok without even cutting off its head and tail. Hold it firmly by the head and tail to press the body down into the center of the pan as it cooks.

1 cod, or sole, or other firm white fish; 12 or 14 inches long with head and tail
2 cups peanut oil for deep frying
1 tsp garlic juice, or 1 clove garlic, minced
1 tsp ginger juice, or 1 tsp ginger root, minced
1 Tbsp green onion, minced
1 tsp salt

Sauce:
2 Tbsp dried mushrooms, soaked, and sliced 1/4 inch wide
2 Tbsp preserved turnip, cut in matchstick slices
2 Tbsp bamboo shoots, cut in matchstick slices
2 Tbsp dark soy sauce
2 tsp sugar
2 cups chicken broth
1 tsp hot oil

Thickener: 1 tsp cornstarch
1/4 cup water

Clean the fish through the gill opening, and score each side with three diagonal slashes.

Heat the oil, and deep fry the fish for 2 minutes on each side. Remove the fish from the wok and pour off the cooking oil. Now put the fish into a pan with a lid (the wok will do unless the fish is too big). Add garlic, ginger root, green onion, and salt first, so they can soak into the fish. Then mix the ingredients of the Sauce and add to the fish. Cover and simmer for 10 minutes.

Remove the fish to a serving dish. Thicken the remaining Sauce with Thickener; pour it over the fish, and serve.

PORK SHOULDER ROAST

Here is a recipe for a savory roast using only the simplest ingredients for its rich flavor.

1 pork shoulder
1 cup soy sauce
2 tsp sugar
2 cloves garlic, sliced

2 medium onions, quartered
1 bunch carrots, cut in chunks
1/2 tsp cornstarch, blended with 1 Tbsp
    water

Roast the meat at 350° for 20 minutes per lb.

Remove to a deep, close-fitting pot; add soy sauce, sugar, and garlic. Simmer for 1/2 hour, turning once. Add the onions and carrots for the last 20 minutes.

While the roast is simmering, add 1/2 cup water to the drippings in the roasting pan, stir and boil them, and thicken them with 1/2 tsp cornstarch and water. Now to this gravy add 1 Tbsp of the soy-sugar-garlic-sauce from the simmering pot. Drain the roast and vegetables, and serve with gravy.

Save the simmering liquid for later sauces.

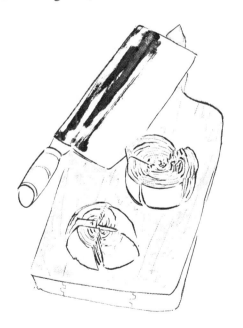

STUFFED BEAN CAKE

4 bean cakes, dried slightly—as in List of
   Chinese Ingredients
2 cups peanut oil for deep frying
Stuffing: 1/2 lb ground pork
               3 Tbsp soy sauce
               1 tsp ginger juice
               3 water chestnuts,
                   minced
               2 Tbsp green onion,
                   minced
               1/2 tsp salt
               2 Tbsp cornstarch
1 Tbsp peanut oil
1 yellow onion, cut lengthwise into
   matchstick strips
1 green pepper, cut into matchstick
   strips
Special Sauce: 1/2 cup chicken broth
               1/4 cup soy sauce
               1 tsp ginger juice

               or: 3/4 cup Basic Sauce
Thickener: 1 tsp cornstarch
               1/2 cup water

Cut each bean cake into 4 cubes and deep fry for about 5 minutes. Turn bean cake until lightly browned on both sides. Drain on paper towels.

Mix the Stuffing. It should be very soft. Add some water if necessary.

With your fingers, poke a hole in a fried bean cake; you will find it is almost empty. Spoon in some stuffing and press the edges back into shape.

Heat a wok, add peanut oil, and stir-fry the onion and pepper for 2 minutes. Add Special Sauce, or Basic Sauce, and the stuffed bean cakes. Simmer 10 minutes.

Open a space in the middle of the pan to put in a little Thickener; stir until smooth, and serve.

ROCK COD

This fish is gently poached then covered with a simple sauce.

1 rock cod, or chunk of rock cod, about
   3 lbs, cleaned
2 tsp salt
2 slices ginger root
2 Tbsp soy sauce
1/4 cup peanut oil
2 tsp ginger strips
6 green onions, white part only, in 2
   inch sections, halved
2 Tbsp cornstarch
1 Tbsp soy sauce

Put enough water into a large pot to cover the fish completely. Bring it to a boil with salt and ginger root. Put in the fish, turn off the heat, and cover the pot. The fish will cook in about 25 minutes; check it with a chopstick to see if the meat slips easily from the backbone.

Place the fish on a platter and immediately sprinkle it with salt inside and out. Spoon over it 2 Tbsp soy sauce mixed with 2 Tbsp broth from the simmering pot.

Heat the peanut oil in a saucepan and add the ginger strips. When they turn light golden, add the green onion sections.

Mix together 2 Tbsp cornstarch with 1/2 cup broth from the simmering pot, and add to the green onion and ginger sauce. Add 1 Tbsp soy sauce. When it is smooth and boiling, pour it over the fish.

CHICKEN STEW WITH CHESTNUTS

2 Tbsp peanut oil
1 slice ginger root
1 fryer, cut to pieces the size of an egg,
   bone and all. If you can buy chicken
   parts, use wings, thighs, and legs only.
1 yellow onion, halved and quartered
1 cup canned chestnuts in heavy syrup,
   quartered*
4 Tbsp dark soy sauce, or 1/2 cup
   Basic Sauce
1-1/2 cup water
Thickener: 1 tsp cornstarch
            1/2 cup water

Heat a wok, add 2 Tbsp peanut oil and a slice of ginger root. Brown the chicken. Add and stir-fry the onion. Add the chestnuts and syrup, soy sauce or Basic Sauce, and water.

Simmer for 20 minutes. Thicken the broth with cornstarch and water. Salt to taste. If it is too sweet, add more salt.

*Available in Oriental stores.

CRISP BEAN THREADS & PORK

Marinade: 2 Tbsp soy sauce
1 tsp ginger juice
1 tsp cornstarch
1/2 lb ground pork
2 Tbsp peanut oil
1 clove garlic, minced
1/2 cup bamboo shoots, diced 1/4
inch cubes
2 tsp preserved pepper, minced
2 cups chicken broth
2 Tbsp dark soy sauce
Thickener: 2 Tbsp cornstarch
1/2 cup water
Salt to taste
4 cups peanut oil for deep frying
2 oz. package bean threads

Mix Marinade and marinate ground pork for 20 minutes.

Heat a frying pan, or wok, add peanut oil, and stir-fry the pork for 3 minutes. Add the garlic, bamboo shoots, and preserved pepper, and stir-fry for 2 more minutes. Add the chicken broth, soy sauce, and Thickener, and stir until it is smooth. Salt to taste. Keep pan or wok at a slow simmer while you deep fry the bean threads.

Heat oil for deep frying to 400°. Have a pair of tongs ready in your hands to turn over the bean threads—unless you are very handy with chopsticks. Drop into the oil the whole 2 oz. package of bean threads. You do not need to unfold them; they are too stiff anyway. They will suddenly puff out: instant cooking! Turn them over with the tongs at once, to cook the other side, then remove and drain on paper. The whole process of deep-frying should take about ten seconds.

Put the bean threads on a serving dish and pour over them the pork and gravy. Serve immediately.

STEAMED EGGS

Custardy eggs with a sweet-sour sauce.

6 oz ground pork or beef
Marinade: 2 Tbsp soy sauce
             2 tsp cornstarch
             1 tsp ginger juice, or
                 ginger root, minced
             1 Tbsp peanut oil
6 eggs
2 cups chicken broth
1 tsp white distilled vinegar
1 tsp salt
1 Tbsp peanut oil
6 water chestnuts, minced
2 Tbsp green onions, minced
4 Tbsp rice vinegar
1 tsp sugar
Thickener: 1 tsp cornstarch
             2 Tbsp soy sauce
             1/2 cup chicken broth

Mix pork or beef with Marinade.

Beat the eggs lightly and gradually add the broth, white vinegar, and salt. Pour into a glass or crockery bowl deep enough to hold both the egg mixture, and the stir-fry you will add to it later. Put the bowl inside a steamer for 15 minutes.

Heat a wok, add 1 Tbsp peanut oil, add the pork or beef. Stir-fry 2 minutes if it is pork; 1/2 minute if it is beef. Add water chestnuts and green onion, stir-fry 1/2 minute. Add rice vinegar and sugar.

Lift bowl from the steamer as soon as the eggs are set.

Add Thickener to the stir-fry; stir and blend, then pour over the eggs.

SWEET & SOUR PORK

The pork in this dish is twice-fried for crispness. You can do the first frying on one day and the second on the next, if that suits your schedule.

1/2 lb lean pork, in chunks 1/2 x 1/2 x 1 inch
Marinade: 1 Tbsp soy sauce
             1/2 tsp salt
             1/2 tsp ginger juice
             1/2 tsp Szechwan pepper

1/2 cup cornstarch
oil for deep frying, 2 inches deep
1 Tbsp peanut oil
1 green pepper, sliced in strips 1/4
   inch wide
Gravy: 1/2 cup juice from the can
           of pineapple
       4 Tbsp catsup
       2 Tbsp vinegar
       2 Tbsp sugar
       1 tsp salt
3 slices canned pineapple, in 1/2 inch
   sections
Thickener: 1/2 tsp cornstarch
           1/2 cup water
1/2 tsp Szechwan pepper

Marinate the pork for 20 minutes or more, then dredge in cornstarch. Shake off any excess cornstarch and deep fry the pork, putting each piece in separately and doing only a few at a time. Turn them over with clean chopsticks, and remove from the cooking oil after 1/2 minute. Drain well. (These fried pieces may be put aside now, if you want to continue cooking the next day.)

Reheat the peanut oil for deep-frying, and fry the pork pieces again, all at once this time. Drain well.

In a wok, heat 1 Tbsp peanut oil and stir-fry the green pepper. Cover and steam it until it is cooked but still crisp, then remove it from the wok. Mix the Gravy ingredients in the same wok.

Add the green pepper & pineapple to the Gravy. Add a little Thickener, and stir until the Gravy is smooth. Add the pork. Serve with Szechwan pepper sprinkled over the top.

SOY RIBS

2 Tbsp peanut oil
1 tsp ginger, minced
2 lbs pork spareribs, in 2 inch pieces
2 Tbsp Bean Sauce*
2 Tbsp water
1-1/2 cups water
3 yellow onions, halved and quartered
1 clove garlic, minced
Thickener: 1 tsp cornstarch
           1/2 cup water

Heat a wok, add peanut oil, and when the oil starts to smoke put in the ginger and spareribs. Brown the ribs.

Push the ribs away from the center of the pan and put in the Bean Sauce. As you stir and cook it add 2 Tbsp water. Stir the ribs and Bean Sauce together, add 1-1/2 cups water, cover and simmer for 20 minutes. Add onions & garlic, and simmer for another 20 minutes.

Mix Thickener. Push the ribs away from the center of the pan and add a little of the Thickener, stirring to keep it smooth. Use only enough Thickener to make a gravy of rather thin consistency, and discard the rest. Salt to taste.

*Bean Sauce, also sold as Yellow Sauce, or Bean Paste, or Yellow Bean Paste. A canned, salty, tasty preparation made from the ubiquitous soybean. Use it to flavor pork or beef dishes, or put it on the table as a dip for vegetables. Remove it from the can as soon as it is opened. It keeps indefinitely in the refrigerator.

TANGERINE PEEL CHICKEN

This is excellent picnic fare, and it will keep for a week. Plan to cook enough for both a hot dish at dinner, and an elegant cold lunch. Extend the cooking time by 10 minutes for the part you plan to set aside, in order to dry it slightly.

1 4-lb chicken, cut into walnut sized
   pieces
Marinade: 1/2 cup orange peel strips
                or
        1/2 cup dried tangerine
          strips*
        1/4 cup soy sauce
        4 dried chili peppers, sliced
        2 tsp ginger strips, or
          1 tsp ginger juice
        2 Tbsp sugar
        2 whole star anise
          (2 tsp broken pieces)
2 cups oil for frying

Mix chicken with Marinade and refrigerate for 24 hours or more.

Fry chicken in oil 1/2 inch deep, or more, for 20 minutes. Salt to taste.

*Imported dried tangerine skin is by far the better choice for the Marinade. Soak it in warm water for 30 minutes, then slice it 1/4 inch wide and mix it with the Marinade. It will be more delicious if you make up the Marinade and set it aside, a week or longer before marinating the chicken.

LION'S HEAD

This traditional dish is so named because the softly shaped meatball looks like a lion's head and the cabbage looks like his ruffled mane.

1 Chinese cabbage
Meatball mix: **2 lbs ground pork**
      1/2 cup water
         chestnuts, chopped
      1/2 cup green onion,
         minced
      1 egg
      3 Tbsp dried shrimp,
         soaked and minced
      1 tsp salt
      4 Tbsp soy sauce
Cornstarch mix: **2 tsp cornstarch**
      1/2 cup water or broth
1 cup chicken broth

Quarter the cabbage, cut crosswise into 1/2 inch slices, and lay it in the bottom of the cooking pot. Blend the Meatball mix. It should be soft.

To form the Meatballs: Pour a Tablespoonful of the Cornstarch mix into your left hand; then a Tablespoonful of the Meatball mix. Turn and form the meatball between the spoon and your left hand, adding more of the Cornstarch mix to coat it. Lay the meatballs on top of the cabbage; they should be soft enough to collapse slightly, and about the size of a duck egg.

Add 1 cup chicken broth to cooking pot; cover, and simmer for 40 minutes.

With a slotted spoon, gently remove the meatballs and cabbage to a serving dish. Add the remaining Cornstarch mix to the broth that is still in the cooking pan; heat and stir until it thickens; pour it over the meatballs and cabbage.

FRIED FISH FILLETS

1 lb fresh fish fillets, in pieces 1-1/2
   inches long and 1/2 inch wide
2 Tbsp ginger juice
1/2 tsp salt
dash ground pepper
1 Tbsp cornstarch
1 egg white, beaten with 1 Tbsp
   cornstarch
oil for deep frying

Brush fillets with ginger juice, then sprinkle salt and pepper on them. Pat them with cornstarch.

Beat egg white with 1 Tbsp cornstarch until mixture is stiff but not dry. Dip fillets in this egg white mixture.

Heat oil, and deep fry fillets until they are done. Do not allow egg white coating to turn brown.

RED DUCK

1/2 fresh duck, cut into bite-sized pieces
1 Tbsp peanut oil
1 slice ginger root
Sauce: 1/4 cup soy sauce
          2 yellow onions, quartered
          3 flowerettes (2 Tbsp) star
            anise
          2 dried chili peppers
          1 tsp ginger root, minced
          1/2 cup water
1 cup bamboo shoots, sliced in thin
    strips 1/4 inch wide
2 Tbsp sugar
Thickener: 1 tsp cornstarch
           1/2 cup water

Remove and discard the section of duck tail with oil glands.

Pan fry the duck in peanut oil with ginger root slice for 5 minutes. Cover pan loosely (so that steam can escape); lower the heat, and steam for 15 minutes. Pour off the fat and discard the ginger slice.

Mix Sauce and add to the duck. Simmer covered 30 minutes. Add bamboo shoots; and simmer 10 minutes longer. Add sugar.

Mix the Thickener; add to the duck and sauce, stirring in a little bit at a time, until the Sauce is slightly thickened.

MANDARIN FRIED RICE

2 or 3 beaten eggs, with a pinch of salt
4 Tbsp cooking fat: ham fat or chicken
    fat or peanut oil
4 or 5 cups cooked rice. (Rice is better
    if one day old.)

4 green onions, chopped
1 cup cooked ham, cut in matchstick
    strips
1 cup cooked peas
2 tsp salt

Note: Any kind of meat, bacon, or sausage is suitable for this dish.

To prepare fresh meat, cut it in fine pieces, marinate in 1 tsp soy sauce, 1/2 tsp ginger juice and 1/2 tsp cornstarch for each 1/4 lb meat; and stir-fry.

To prepare bacon, mince, and stir-fry lightly.

To prepare Chinese sausage, cut in cubes and steam for 10 minutes.

Scramble the eggs at a low-moderate heat in 1 Tbsp cooking fat just long enough so they are cooked but so soft they fall apart when added to the rice. Eggs must not be browned. Remove from wok.

Heat wok, add 3 Tbsp cooking fat, and stir in the rice (If the rice is cold, add 1/2 cup water and cover the wok to steam it for a minute or two.)

Stirring continually, add the green onion, cooked ham, or other prepared meat, eggs, peas, and salt. Serve when heated.

TEA EGGS

Bring tea eggs in their shells to a picnic. Or offer them as hors d'oeuvres, shelled & quartered. Shelled tea eggs have a beautiful brown crackle pattern.

1 dozen eggs
Broth: 2 Tbsp black tea leaves
   1 Tbsp star anise (about three
    whole flowerettes)
   2 Tbsp salt
   5 cups water, or more: enough
    to cover

Simmer eggs 10 minutes, then plunge them into cold water.

Tap each egg so that it is lightly cracked all over.

Combine cracked eggs and Broth; simmer for two hours. Leave them to cool in the Broth overnight. Discard the Broth, and serve the tea eggs either cold or at room temperature.

CHAPTER VI

CHINESE FLOUR ART

All is not rice. There is also the flour art: noodles, dumplings, and spring rolls. Noodles may be eaten plain, or in soup, or roasted, or with a spicy sauce. They are good for any occasion, and especially a birthday party. Long life to you!

Dumplings and wrapped meats of various kinds may be simmered, steamed, or fried. Here are recipes for sauteed dumplings (Potstickers), deep-fried and simmered dumplings (Spring Roll and Won Ton), and a sauteed Onion Cake.

To do some of the cooking ahead of time, you can parboil and roast the noodles the day before you plan to simmer them. Cover lightly, to store. The meat fillings for dumplings may be made and refrigerated for a day, before using them. Notice that fillings must be very moist. They may be further softened with water if necessary, unless they are to be stored; in that case soften them with oil. Dough tends to dry out very fast, so cover up the part you are not handling. Dumplings of all kinds must be cooked within an hour or two after they are made.

The Chinese art of flour arranging consists in getting your friends to help you. How do you do that? You say, "Come over and help me wrap won ton." Not very artful, but what a good beginning for a party!

ROASTED NOODLES

These roasted noodles are far superior to those in the standard Ameri-can Chow Mein.

1 lb fresh noodles*
1/4 cup peanut oil
2 cans (approx. 4 cups) chicken broth

Bring 3 quarts of water to a boil, add 1/2 tsp peanut oil; separate the noodles as you drop them in, so they don't stick together. Bring to a boil again, and boil them for 3 minutes. Turn them out in a colander to drain.

Pour peanut oil into a baking pan 8 by 12 inches, or larger. Put in the noodles, stir to coat them with oil, and spread them out evenly over the bottom of the pan. Bake in an oven at 350 until they are lightly brown on top and bottom, but are still moist in the middle, about 40 minutes. Now put them into a saucepan with 1/4 cup chicken broth, cover, and simmer for 20 minutes, adding the rest of the chicken broth, 1/2 cup at a time, as liquid is needed.

Turn them out on a large platter and sprinkle over them the following Topping for Roasted Noodles.

*If you are using dried egg noodles, follow the directions for cooking on the package, but cook them only half as long.

TOPPING FOR ROASTED NOODLES

1/2 lb pork, cut in matchstick strips
Marinade: 2 Tbsp soy sauce
               2 tsp cornstarch
               1 tsp ginger juice
2 Tbsp peanut oil
1 cup celery, sliced 1/8 inch
1/2 cup green onion, matchstick strips
1 lb bean sprouts, blanched in boiling
   water
1 cup preserved turnip, matchstick strips
Salt to taste
1/2 bunch Chinese parsley leaves

Marinate the pork.

Heat a wok, add 1 Tbsp peanut oil, and stir-fry the celery for 1/2 minute; cover and steam for 1 minute. Remove from pan.

Stir-fry the green onions and bean sprouts together for 1 minute. Remove from pan.

Heat 1 Tbsp peanut oil, add the pork and stir-fry for 1 minute. Add the preserved turnip and stir-fry together for 2 minutes. Now add the celery, green onions, and bean sprouts, and stir-fry just long enough to heat them, salt to taste, and spoon them over the noodles.

Garnish with Chinese parsley leaves.

CHINESE RAVIOLI (WON TON)

Meat Filling: 1 lb ground pork
1 egg
1/4 cup soy sauce
1/4 cup peanut oil
2 Tbsp sesame oil
1 tsp ginger juice
1/4 cup dried mush-
    rooms, soaked &
    chopped
4 or 5 water chestnuts,
    minced
1/2 cup green onions,
    chopped
1/2 tsp salt
1 lb prepared won ton skins, or roll your own (see Potsticker dough, page 102. and cut into 3 inch squares)
1 bunch spinach, washed and cut 3 inches long
1 can chicken broth (approximately 2 cups)
3 cans of water

Blend together Meat Filling. It should be very moist. Add 1 Tbsp of oil, or more, if necessary.

Put 1 rounded tsp of Meat Filling on a won ton skin, fold once to make a triangle and press the edges together to seal. Dip a chopstick into water and touch the edge to make it stick.

Bring chicken broth and water to a gentle boil and drop won ton in, one by one. Simmer 3 minutes. Add spinach on top of won ton, simmer 3 more minutes, and serve.

Here is the way to wrap won ton. The result is not a neat package with the edges tucked in—in fact, the edges will stick out like the fins and tail of a very ornamental goldfish.

1. Lay 1/2 tsp filling on the corner of a won ton skin and roll it up to the center.

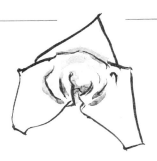

4. Now pull the two angles down South toward·each other. Don't twist them to do this; they should remain flat.

2. Now you have a triangle, with an angle at East and West, and a right angle at the North. Keep it flat like a map.

5. Pinch them together overlapping, with a dot of water to make them stick.
When you get the knack of it, you will say—why did it take all that explanation?

But if you still don't see how it is done, you can wrap your won ton like an apple turnover, with one fold and a squeeze (and a bit of moisture to make it stick).

3. Pinch the East and West angles close to the filling, to hold the filling in.

POTSTICKERS

Meat Filling: 1 1/2 lbs ground pork
6 Tbsp soy sauce
6 green onions, minced
2 Tbsp dried shrimp,
    soaked and minced
3 Tbsp of the "shrimp
    water"
1 Tbsp sesame oil
2 Tbsp peanut oil
1 tsp ginger juice
1 egg
1 Chinese cabbage, 1 to 1-1/2 lb
2 tsp salt
5 cups flour and 2 cups water (This makes 40 potstickers)

Blend the Meat Filling.

Discard the core of the Chinese cabbage, and cut the rest into 1/4 inch slices.

Put it in a bowl and sprinkle with 2 tsp salt. Knead it with your hands, and press out as much juice as possible. Add cabbage to the Meat Filling. The filling should be very soft; if it is not, add 1 Tbsp peanut oil or more.

Mix the flour and water. Keep it rather soft for greater ease in working. Knead it for a few minutes, then let the dough rest for 10 minutes.

Roll out the dough, then roll it up into a one-inch thick cylinder. Cut the cylinder into 3/4 inch pieces. Roll each piece out into a little pancake 3 or 4 inches across. Give an extra pressing to the edges, so they are thinner than the middle.

Put a full tsp of Meat Filling in the middle of the pancake and close it up, pleating one edge of the closing so the potsticker is crescent-shaped. Put a dot of water on the edge before you close it, if the dough is too dry to stick together.

Heat a frying pan, oil it, and lay the potstickers close together with the pleated side up. Saute for a few minutes. Watch them carefully, because they burn easily. Add 1/2 cup water to the pan, cover, and steam for 20 minutes. Potstickers are turned over only once—into the serving dish, where they show the browned side.

Serve them with several condiments on the table: hot oil and vinegar, soy sauce and Chinese parsley.

Chinese
Parsley
coriander

ONION CAKE

These crisp, delicious pancakes are much favored by the young, who gobble them up as fast as they come from the frying pan. You may divide the cooking time for your own convenience: roll out and lightly pan fry the onion cakes early in the afternoon, cool and set them aside, then brown them later on.

Dough: **2 1/2 cups flour**
             3/4 to 1 cup water
4 Tbsp chicken fat, bacon fat, or
   rendered lard, chilled
1 cup green onion, chopped
1 cup bacon, minced
1 tsp salt
2 Tbsp peanut oil

Mix the dough and knead it for 10 minutes. Let it "rest" while you prepare the other ingredients.

Roll out the dough with a rolling pin until it is about 1/8 inch thick. Spread the chicken, or bacon fat, or lard, on top of it with a pastry brush, then sprinkle over it the minced bacon and chopped green onion. Sprinkle salt generously.

Roll the dough up tight into a long solid cylinder, and cut it into 4 sections. Pick up each section and pinch the ends so that the fat does not run out. Now take one end in each hand and twist and press it toward the other end, so that you have a flat pancake between your palms. Put it down on a piece of wax paper and roll it out to about 6 inches in diameter. Use as little extra flour as possible.

Heat a flat-bottomed pan, add 2 Tbsp peanut oil. Pan-fry over medium heat until brown on both sides. Remove from pan, and let stand a minute; then slice into pie-shaped pieces.

SZECHWAN SAUCE AND NOODLES

1 lb ground pork
Marinade: 1/4 cup soy sauce
            2 tsp cornstarch
            1 tsp ginger juice
2 Tbsp peanut oil
2 cloves garlic, minced
1 medium yellow onion, chopped
1/3 cup yellow bean paste*
1/2 cup preserved turnip, cut in matchstick strips
2 cups chicken stock
2 tsp sugar
Salt to taste
1 lb fresh noodles or dried noodles
1 tsp peanut oil
Thickener: 1 tsp cornstarch
            1/4 cup water

Garnish: 3 Tbsp green onion,
             chopped
            1 tsp hot oil
            1 Tbsp sesame oil

Mix pork and Marinade. Heat a wok, add peanut oil. Add and stir-fry the garlic and onion until lightly browned. Then add in order: pork, bean paste, preserved turnip, chicken stock, and sugar. Cover and simmer for 10 minutes. Salt to taste.

Boil noodles for 5 or 6 minutes, with peanut oil. Turn into colander and then into serving dish. (If dried noodles are used, cook according to package directions.)

Add Thickener to pork sauce and stir. Serve sauce in a serving dish with green onion, hot oil, and sesame oil sprinkled over it.

*See page 88

SPRING ROLL

1/2 lb pork, cut in thin strips
Marinade: 3 Tbsp soy sauce
                1 tsp wine
                2 tsp cornstarch
                1/4 cup water
2 Tbsp peanut oil
1/2 cup bamboo shoots, cut in match-
    stick strips
4 to 6 dried mushrooms, soaked, cut in
    1/4 inch strips
1/4 lb bean sprouts
3 green onions, in 2 inch sections, cut
    in fine shreds
Salt to taste
Thickener: 2 tsp cornstarch
                1/4 cup water
10 prepared spring roll pancake rounds,
    9-inch diameter. If these are not avail-
    able, make a dough of flour and water
    as in the Potstickers, and roll it out
    into rounds.
Oil for deep frying

Mix pork and Marinade.

Heat a wok, add peanut oil, and stir-fry the pork for 3 minutes. Add bamboo shoots and mushrooms, and continue to stir-fry for 3 minutes. Add bean sprouts and onions. Salt to taste. Then pour a little of the cornstarch and water into the middle of the pan; when it thickens, mix it with the ingredients. Refrigerate for 20 minutes.

Put 2 Tbsp of the filling in the middle of a spring roll round. Fold the dough over it from the bottom, then from the left side, then from the right; then finish rolling it up from the bottom like a long envelope. Seal the flap with a drop of cornstarch-and-water, and gently press edge.

Fry in deep fat until golden brown, turning once.

CHAPTER VII

CHINESE VEGETABLES

Flavor and freshness in vegetables are conserved by Chinese cooking methods. Quick stir-frying with high heat cooks vegetables to just the right degree of crisp tenderness. Chinese cooks also have ways with vinegar and brine that protect the consistency of vegetables.

This chapter serves up a variety of delectable vegetable dishes, both hot and cold, as well as two kinds of Chinese chicken salad. Also included is a word or two about the most exotic and popular Chinese vegetables—even though many of them are more common to South than North China. With the increasing interest in Oriental cooking, a number of these exotic vegetables are becoming available in regular produce markets.

With any of these recipes, however, feel free to substitute the vegetables that are available to you. As long as you use the Chinese seasonings, you can cook any vegetables with an Oriental accent.

TART RADISHES

Here are marinated radishes with a new and different flavor! Serve them as appetizers before dinner.

2 bunches red radishes
Marinade: 2 Tbsp distilled white
                    vinegar
                  3 Tbsp sugar
2 tsp sesame oil
sugar

Crack the radishes this way: lay them on a cutting board and strike lightly with the side of a cleaver.

Mix with Marinade and refrigerate overnight. Before serving, drain them and stir in sesame oil, and sweeten with sugar to taste.

STUFFED EGGPLANT

Stuffing: 1/4 lb ground pork
1 egg, beaten lightly
2 tsp cornstarch
3 Tbsp green onion, minced
5 water chestnuts, minced
2 Tbsp soy sauce
1/2 tsp salt
3 large eggplants, sliced into "buns"
4 Tbsp peanut oil
1 cup water or meat stock
1/4 cup soy sauce
1 clove garlic, minced
3 Tbsp sugar
Thickener: 1/2 tsp cornstarch
1/4 cup water or broth
Salt to taste

Mix together the stuffing ingredients.

Make "buns" of the eggplant this way: put the eggplant on a cutting board and lay a chopstick on either side of it. Using a cleaver or a knife with a straight blade, slice the eggplant into 1/2 inch slices. The two parallel chopsticks will prevent the knife blade from slicing all the way through the eggplant. Now put aside the chopsticks and cut through every other slice, so that you have 4 or 5 "buns" from each eggplant. Fill them with stuffing.

Heat a flat-bottomed pan. Add peanut oil. Brown the eggplant buns on both sides. You may need to add more oil to keep them from burning. They turn dark-brown.

Add the water or meat stock, soy sauce, garlic, and sugar. Cover and simmer for 15 minutes. Lift one of the buns from the middle of the pan so that you have room to stir in the Thickener; add Thickener a little at a time, stirring, until the sauce is smooth and of medium thickness.

Salt to taste.

Chinese Okra is a green luffa gourd. It has a bland, cool flavor. Slice off the long, sharp edges, and cut into chunks for soup, or add it to stir-fry dishes.

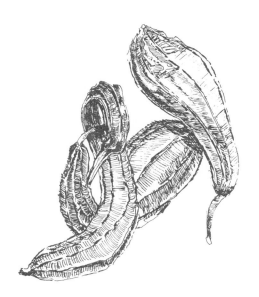

Bean Sprouts grow from mung or soy beans. To preserve their delicate flavor and crisp consistency, avoid soaking them. To eat them fresh, as in a salad, dip in boiling water. To cook them, stir-fry for 1 minute only.

CUCUMBER STEW

2 medium or large cucumbers
1/2 tsp hot oil
1 tsp peanut oil
Sauce: 2 tsp soy sauce
           2 tsp sugar
           1 Tbsp vinegar
Thickener: 1/2 tsp cornstarch
           1/2 cup water
Salt to taste

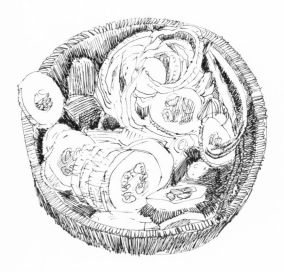

Slice cucumbers in half lengthwise. Spoon out and discard the seeds. Cut into 1/4 inch slices.

Heat a wok. Add hot oil and peanut oil. Stir-fry the cucumber slices for about 2 minutes. Add the Sauce, turn the heat down to low; cover and steam for 5 minutes.

Push the cucumbers away from the center of the wok, and add the Thickener, stirring. Salt to taste. When the sauce is smooth and thick, remove to a serving dish.

MUSHROOM CABBAGE

2 Tbsp peanut oil
1 medium-sized cabbage, sliced in 1 x 2
   inch squares
1 tsp salt
1/2 cup chicken stock
1/2 cup dried mushrooms, soaked,
   sliced 1/4 inch wide
Thickener: 1 tsp cornstarch
             1/2 cup chicken stock

Heat a wok, add peanut oil, and stir-fry the cabbage for 1/2 minute. Add salt, chicken stock, and mushrooms; simmer covered for 10 minutes.

Push the cabbage away from the center of the wok, and pour in a little of the Thickener, stirring as it heats. Add only as much Thickener as it takes to give a small quantity of sauce; discard the rest. Stir the cabbage and sauce together, and serve immediately.

SWEET & SOUR BROCCOLI PICKLES

This is an appetizer that used to be served to the men while the women were busy preparing dinner. Since women's lib, it's anybody's appetizer!

1 lb broccoli, stems only
Marinade: 2 Tbsp distilled white
                vinegar
            1 tsp salt
            2 Tbsp sugar
2 Tbsp sesame oil

Peel broccoli stems completely. Slice each stem in half lengthwise, lay the cut side down for easier handling, and make diagonal slices 1/8 inch thick.

Mix Marinade in a refrigerator storage jar, add broccoli slices, stir or shake, and refrigerate overnight.

Use a slotted spoon to drain them, and put them in a serving dish, and pour sesame oil over them.

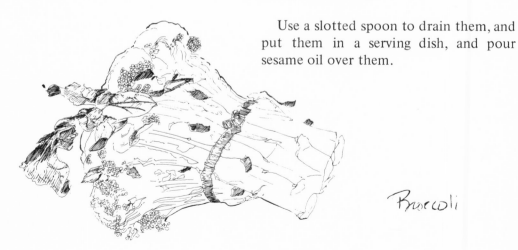

Broccoli

COOL CHICKEN SALAD

1 whole chicken breast
1/2 lb fresh bean sprouts
Dressing: 4 Tbsp soy sauce
             3 Tbsp vinegar
             2 Tbsp sesame oil
             1 tsp ginger juice
             2 Tbsp sugar
             2 tsp dry mustard
             2 tsp hot oil
             1 tsp Szechwan pepper
             1 clove garlic, crushed
             1/2 tsp salt
1/2 cup jellyfish*, soaked and cut in
  1/4 inch strips
Garnish: 1/4 cup green onions,
              minced
             1/4 cup Chinese-parsley
             1/4 cup sesame seeds,
              roasted

Cut the chicken breast in two. Drop the two halves into boiling salted water and immediately turn off the heat, cover the pot, and set it aside for 20 minutes. Drain the chicken breast, let it cool enough to handle, and then shred it with your fingers into pieces about 1/8 inch thick and as long as possible. Cut the skin into 1/8 inch slices.

Parboil the bean sprouts for 1/2 minute, drain and rinse.

Mix the Dressing, and in a large bowl; combine Dressing with chicken skin, chicken, bean sprouts, and jellyfish.

Garnish salad with green onions, parsley and sesame seeds.

*jellyfish is not what the name implies. See page 11 .

Oriental Eggplant is purple or white, and thinner and less seedy than the pear-shaped variety.

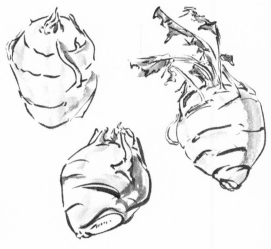

Kohlrabi has an edible, bulbous stem. Like the jicama, it is white, crisp, sweet, and delicate in flavor. Peel and slice it, and eat it raw or add it to stir-fried dishes.

CHILLED EGGPLANT

The proper eggplant for this is the little thin kind, either purple or white, generally found in Oriental markets. The bigger and rounder type more often seen in Western markets will do almost as well, however.

```
1 lb eggplants
Dressing:    3 Tbsp vinegar
             2 Tbsp sugar
             4 Tbsp soy sauce
             2 Tbsp sesame oil
             1 garlic clove, quartered
             2 slices ginger root
             1/2 tsp black pepper
             1/2 tsp hot oil
             1 green onion, minced
             1/2 tsp salt
Garnish:     Chinese parsley
```

Boil the eggplants whole and unpeeled, for 30 minutes. Cut in half lengthwise and turn them cut side down in a colander so they can drain as they cool.

Mix the ingredients for the Dressing and set it aside to blend.

Put the eggplant halves in a covered bowl, and pour over the Dressing and refrigerate for several hours or overnight.

When it is time to serve the eggplant, gently cut it into long, thin sections, and arrange it on a serving dish. Strain the Dressing and pour over it. Garnish with Chinese parsley.

Snow Peas, or sugar peas, are edible pea pods, sweet and crisp. They keep well in the refrigerator vegetable compartment. Pinch off each end, and add the pods to any stir-fried dish for the last two minutes of cooking.

Long Beans, or yard long beans, may be cooked like string beans: pinch off the ends, slice, and stir-fry.

SWEET & SOUR CHICKEN SALAD

1 fresh frying chicken, cut in half
1 tsp salt
4 slices ginger root
green onion tops
1/2 cup green onion, in matchstick
    slices
1/2 cup canned preserved ginger, sliced
    fine
1/2 cup canned pickled scallions,
    quartered*

Dressing: 1/4 cup soy sauce
              1/4 cup vinegar
              2 Tbsp sesame oil
              2 Tbsp sugar
              2 tsp dry mustard
              1 tsp chili paste or hot oil
              1 tsp ginger juice

Garnish: 1/4 cup Chinese parsley
              leaves

Salt the chicken then put it cut-side down in a shallow bowl suitable for placing in a steamer. Lay on top of the chicken the slices of ginger root, and several green onion tops. Steam the chicken for 30 minutes, according to directions for steaming, page 23 . Let chicken cool to room temperature while you prepare the other ingredients.

Pull the chicken from its bones with your fingers, shredding it into pieces about 1/4 inch square and as long as the fiber allows. Save the skin—it is a delicacy; slice it into strips 1/8 inch wide, and add it to the salad.

Mix the chicken, green onion, ginger, scallions, and Dressing in a large bowl. Sprinkle over Chinese parsley.

*Available in oriental markets.

WHITE RADISH SALAD

The Chinese white radish looks like a giant, white carrot. It is one of the commonest vegetables in Oriental markets.

2 Chinese white radishes (2 lbs)
1/4 cup distilled white vinegar
1 Tbsp salt
Dressing: 1/4 cup soy sauce
                1 tsp ginger root, minced
                1 tsp dry mustard
                1 Tbsp sesame oil
                1 tsp hot oil
                3 Tbsp sugar
                2 green onions, minced
Garnish: 1 bunch Chinese parsley
                leaves

Peel radishes. Slice diagonally, then into matchstick strips. Stir in vinegar and salt and cover radishes very closely because they have a strong aroma. Marinate overnight.

Drain and squeeze vegetables to remove vinegar. Mix with Dressing and garnish with parsley. If it is too salty, add more vinegar.

White Radish, also called Chinese turnip or daikon, looks like a giant, white carrot. It may be grated or sliced fine, and eaten raw with a vinegar sauce, or cooked in soups or stir-fried dishes.

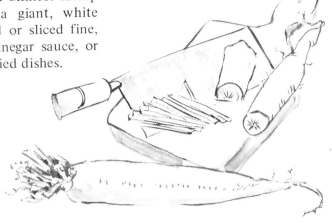

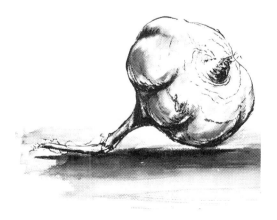

Jicama (Hee-Kah-Ma), a root vegetable, looks like a very fat turnip. The skin may be pulled off after an initial knife cut. The flesh is white, sweet, and crisp. It may be sliced fine and eaten raw, or diced and added to stir-fried dishes.

HOT CABBAGE

1 Chinese cabbage, about 2 lbs, stems
   only
2 tsp salt
1 Tbsp peanut oil
1/2 tsp Szechwan peppercorns
3 preserved chili peppers, minced
Sauce: 2 Tbsp sugar
               2 Tbsp vinegar
               1 tsp sesame oil
               2 tsp ginger juice

Slice cabbage stems lengthwise 1/2 inch wide and 2 inches long. Sprinkle with salt, stir, and set aside for 30 minutes. Press out the moisture with your hands, and pat dry with a paper towel.

Heat a wok, add the peanut oil, and brown the peppercorns until they are dark. Add the chili peppers, and cabbage stems, and stir-fry for three minutes. Add the Sauce, stir-fry 1/2 minute more, and serve.

SWEET & SOUR CABBAGE

1 small or medium-sized head cabbage,
   quartered, sliced 1 inch wide
2 Tbsp peanut oil
Sauce: 1/2 cup vinegar
               2 Tbsp soy sauce
               2 Tbsp sugar
               1 Tbsp hot oil
Salt to taste

Mix the Sauce.

Rinse the cabbage in a colander, and dry it.

Heat a wok, add peanut oil, and stir-fry cabbage until it is cooked but still slightly crisp. Stir in the Sauce, salt to taste, and serve.

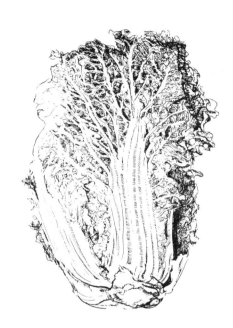

Chinese Cabbage, Pe-Ts'ai, Napa, or celery cabbage, looks like a white, elongated cabbage. Its flavor is light and tart. It keeps well in the refrigerator vegetable compartment; it may be stir-fried, steamed, or added to soup; and in general it is a most useful and delicious Chinese vegetable.

Bok Choy is a cabbage that looks like Swiss chard. It has a delicate flavor, and requires light cooking: slice the stems in 1 inch sections, stir-fry for 2 minutes. Add the leaves for 1/4 minute only.

MUSTARD GREENS SALAD

The spiciness in this Chinese vegetable is developed by heating it on the stove, then closing it up tight in a container overnight. When you serve it cold, the flavor is hot!

1 Tbsp peanut oil
1 lb tender mustard greens, cut in 1 inch
   squares
Dressing: 1 tsp salt
                 1 Tbsp soy sauce
                 2 tsp sesame oil
                 1 Tbsp vinegar
                 1 Tbsp sugar

Heat a wok, add 1 Tbsp peanut oil. When the oil is smoky, add the mustard and stir quickly for a few seconds. Pop the mustard into a sterilized container with a tight lid and close it immediately. Set it aside for a few hours, or overnight.

Mix the Dressing and add it to the mustard. Let it stand for 1 or 2 hours more before serving.

Bitter Melon is a green balsam pear. It has a cool, bitter, refreshing flavor. Slice it lengthwise, remove and discard the seeds, and slice crosswise in 1/4 inch sections. May be parboiled for 2 minutes to reduce the sharp taste. Stir-fry with beef slices and black bean sauce.

Wintermelon is a giant squash, bigger and fatter than a watermelon, with frosty green skin and cool white flesh. It is cut and sold by the piece in Chinese markets for soup making.

CHAPTER VIII

SOUP

LAST

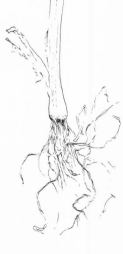

"Beautiful soup, so rich and green
Waiting in a hot tureen . . ."

sang the Mock Turtle, doubtless referring to Seaweed Soup. An electric
wok, or electric skillet, is even more useful than a tureen, for keeping
soup hot at the table. Then it can be eaten in the Chinese style; that is,
as a side dish with dinner—or after dinner.

In some of the following recipes, soup is made with canned chicken
broth. Canned broth is light in flavor, it is handy, it saves time; it has
many virtues. But if you choose to make your own broth, instead, you
can control the saltiness, and be more thrifty, too. In the Chinese kitchen,
nothing is wasted, nothing is thrown away. Water that was used to soak
the dried mushrooms, dried shrimp, trimmings from the chicken gizzards, stems of parsley—each will yield up its last measure of flavor and
vitamins before it is discarded. For instance, to make a little light broth
to drink with dinner instead of the ubiquitous tea: combine in a bowl
some pork liver trimmings, a slice of ginger root, the top of a green
onion, and some water and a pinch of salt. Place the bowl inside a
steamer for a few hours.

Or shall we begin with bones? Take chicken bones or pork bones, or
both together. Cover with water, add a pinch of salt, and a slice of ginger
root and onion, bring to a boil, and skim the top. Simmer for two hours
Strain, and refrigerate.

OXTAIL SOUP

More tomatoes may be added to this soup. They give it a beautiful color and mingle well with the oxtail flavor. The onion and celery should not be overcooked, but still firm. If simplest things are best, then this must be the best soup.

1 oxtail (about 1-1/2 lb), sectioned
1/2 inch slice of ginger root
6 cups water
4 tomatoes, quartered
2 yellow onions, quartered
1-1/2 cup celery, sliced 1/2 inch
Salt to taste

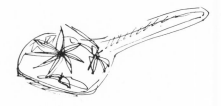

Put oxtail and ginger root in a soup pot with about 6 cups of water and bring to a boil.

Skim the soup carefully at least once, as soon as it begins to boil. When the liquid is clear, add tomatoes and simmer for 2-1/2 hours.

Add onions and celery, and simmer for 20 minutes longer. Salt to taste.

HOT AND SOUR SOUP

In addition to the pork you can make excellent use of a little leftover cooked meat in this Hot and Sour Soup. Add it at the same time as the bean cake.

1 oz. pork, sliced thinly
Marinade: 1 Tbsp soy sauce
             1 tsp cornstarch
             1 tsp ginger juice
1 Tbsp peanut oil
1/2 cup clouds' ears, soaked and sliced
1/2 cup bamboo shoots, in matchstick
   slices
1 can (approximately 2 cups) chicken
   broth, and 1 can of water
1/4 cup soy sauce
3 Tbsp vinegar
1 bean cake, in matchstick slices
2 eggs, lightly beaten, with a pinch of salt
Salt to taste

Mix pork with Marinade.

Heat a wok, add peanut oil, and stir-fry the pork slices for 3 minutes.

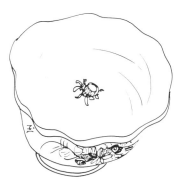

Add clouds' ears and bamboo shoots, and stir briefly. Add broth and water, and simmer for 5 minutes.

Add soy sauce, vinegar, and bean cake. Heat the soup to simmering again, and pour in the beaten egg as you stir it. Salt to taste.

WINTERMELON SOUP WITH MEATBALLS

In the Chinese scheme of things, wintermelon is cool and soothing. Coolness, like vitamins, is found mainly in the skin, so do not discard the peeled skin until it has been simmered in the soup.

1 lb fresh wintermelon, peeled, cut in chunks 1/2 inch square, and the green peelings
3 dried mushrooms, soaked, in 1/4 inch slices
2 cups chicken broth, with 2 cups water

Meatball Mix: 1/2 lb ground pork
3 Tbsp soy sauce
2 Tbsp cornstarch
1/4 tsp salt
1 green onion, minced
1 Tbsp cornstarch in 1/2 cup water

Simmer melon, mushrooms, broth, peelings, and water together for 15 minutes, while you blend the Meatball Mix.

Meatballs should be very soft: if necessary, add a few tablespoonsful of broth from the soup pot. To form the meatballs: Pour a teaspoonful of the cornstarch and water into the palm of your left hand; then add one teaspoonful of the Meatball Mix. Turn and form the meatball between the teaspoon and your left hand, adding more of the cornstarch and water to coat it. These meatballs are small—one teaspoonful of mix is enough for each one.

Add meatballs to the soup for 10 minutes. When they float to the top, they are done. Discard the peelings before you serve the soup.

SEAWEED

SOUP

2 sheets dried seaweed, soaked
1 Tbsp dried shrimp, soaked and minced
1 tsp ginger root, minced
4 cups chicken broth
4 water chestnuts, sliced
1 egg, lightly beaten
Salt to taste

Simmer the seaweed, shrimp, ginger root, in the broth for 20 minutes.

Add the water chestnuts and bring to a boil.

Turn off the heat. Stir in the egg. Salt to taste, and serve.

CONGEE

Any time of the day is the proper time to eat congee. It can be a late-night snack, or a Chinese breakfast, or a lunch or dinner. Congee is a wonderfully tasty rice-gruel, with the additions of meat and fish.

Serve congee at the table, from the electric wok or skillet. Each diner helps himself to some beef slices from a side dish, and then to some congee, and then to a slice of fish on top of that. The heat of the rice-gruel cooks the finely sliced meat and fish right in the bowl.

The bowls should be small, so that congee can be eaten Chinese-style: Hold the bowl up with one hand so that you can drink out of it, and hold your chopsticks in the other hand to pick up the meat and fish slices. Then you can savor it properly.

1 cup rice
6 cups water

Wash the rice well, then put it in a big pot with water and simmer for 3 hours or more. Transfer the rice to an electric wok or skillet. Add more water to keep a soupy consistency.

This process may be speeded with a blender if you start with cooked rice: put 2 cups cooked rice and 2 cups water in a blender at low speed for 1/2 minute. Then pour it into an electric wok or skillet, with 2 cups water, and simmer it for about 20 minutes while you prepare the special things to eat with the congee.

1/4 lb beef, flank steak, sliced very thin
1/2 lb very fresh, firm red tuna, or other very fresh fish; sliced very thin
Marinade: 1 egg white, beaten
2 tsp cornstarch
1 tsp ginger juice, or 1 tsp ginger root, minced, and 1 tsp Chinese wine
1/2 tsp salt
1 tsp sesame oil

Stir some Marinade into beef and fish, and place both bowls next to the hot congee.

With the meat and fish on the table, there should be a bowl of minced green onion, some Chinese parsley, and some pickley, salty, tasty things in side dishes such as:

preserved turnip, minced
pickled scallions
preserved pickled ginger
preserved bean curd

All these can be purchased in Oriental markets.

CHAPTER IX

CELESTIAL

DESSERTS

All sorts of sweet things; cookies, cakes, sweet drinks, and sugary concoctions, are made to be eaten between meals, or at odd hours of the day, or late at night—or whenever a yearning for sweetness overcomes one. But not after dinner, in the Chinese scheme of things.

After dinner is a time for sitting around the cleared table, a time for conversation, a little tea, and a choice of fresh fruit; oranges, pears, and apples, to peel at leisure—or a dish of steamed kumquats.

Celestial desserts, fit for an emperor are still savored—but not always as desserts. So try these sweet treats: Oriental rice pudding, sesame ball (sometimes deep-fried and known as Chinese doughnuts), sweet dessert soup, and steamed kumquats. They're too good to miss; have them for afternoon snacks, or a midnight refreshment.

EIGHT JEWEL RICE PUDDING

Bright-colored bits of fruit decorate the top of this beautiful molded rice dish.

1 lb (2 cups) sweet rice
4 cups water
3/4 cup sugar
2 Tbsp peanut oil
About 1 mixed cup fruits and nuts, cut into small pieces
Choose from any of the following:
    dates, raisins, candied fruit, melon, ginger, blanched and slivered almonds, chestnuts, walnuts, canned ginko nuts

Soaking the rice is not necessary here, but it must be boiled before it goes into the mold. Wash the rice, drain it, and bring it to a boil in 4 cups water. Simmer for 10 minutes, add sugar and peanut oil, and simmer 5 minutes longer.

Oil a shallow bowl or 1-1/2 quart ring mold. Arrange a selection of dried or glaceed fruit, and nuts, in the bottom of it. Fill it with rice. Steam inside a steamer for 3 hours.

This sticky rice does not come out of its mold easily. Run a knife blade around the edges to help separate it. Insert a very long spatula to loosen the bottom surface. Now hold a plate against the bowl and turn it over. Good luck!

Serve warm.

This pudding may be frozen, either before or after steaming. If frozen before steaming, steam it for 3 hours. If steamed and then frozen, warm it for 1 hour in the steamer.

SESAME BALL

1 cup black or white sesame seeds,
    roasted and cooled
1/2 cup walnut meats
1-1/2 cups sugar
1 cup vegetable shortening
1 pkg (1 lb) sweet rice flour and about
    1-1/4 cups water

Mix together in the blender, or mash in a mortar, the sesame seeds and walnuts, and turn them into a bowl. Mix them with sugar and shortening, and form into balls about the diameter of a nickel. Refrigerate them.

Set 1/2 cup rice flour aside to dust the kneading board and your hands. Stir water into the remaining rice flour to form a very soft dough. Knead for 10 minutes, then wrap the dough in wax paper or plastic wrap and let it rest for 10 minutes. Set a pot of water boiling with 1-1/2 quarts water or more.

Pinch off some dough and form a ball about the diameter of a quarter. Poke a hole in it with your finger, then form it into a small cup. Put a sesame ball inside it and gently pull and form the dough around it, compressing it at the top so that the ball is completely and evenly covered with dough. When you have made several balls, start to cook them, because the dough quickly dries out in the air. Keep the dough you are working on covered with plastic wrap as much as possible.

Stir the boiling water in a strong circular motion, and drop in several sesame balls. Give the pot a stir now and then so the balls won't stick to the bottom. They will rise to the top after a few minutes: simmer them for two minutes longer. (Since you are adding more sesame balls to the pot while the earlier ones are cooking, you can't always be sure which ones have cooked exactly 2 minutes—in that case, it will not hurt to cook them longer.)

Remove Sesame Balls from the pot directly into individual small bowls, with 3 to each serving. Spoon several tablespoonsful of the hot water into each bowl. Serve hot.

If any of sesame filling is left over, it may be kept in the refrigerator, and used another time in making Sesame Balls. If any dough is left over, you can make little balls of it, the diameter of a dime and boil them like the sesame balls. These may be eaten warm, sprinkled with the following sesame sugar.

SESAME SUGAR

1 cup roasted sesame seeds
1/2 cup sugar

Spin together in a blender at low speed for 5 seconds. Stir it down. Spin again at low speed for 10 seconds. Or else mash the seeds in a mortar and add sugar. Store in a covered jar.

This sesame sugar also makes a delicious topping for pudding, cereal, or rice, to be eaten late at night, or at breakfast.

ALMOND TEA

Almond Tea is not tea but a sweet dessert soup served in a small bowl. It's exotic, but worth trying.

1/2 cup raw almonds, blanched and skinned
1/2 cup roasted sesame seeds
1/2 cup rice flour
Sugar to taste

Dry roast the almonds over moderate heat, stirring constantly, until they are lightly brown.

Blend almonds, sesame seeds, and rice flour together in a blender at low speed, stopping frequently to stir. Put it through ı medium mesh strainer to make sure it is pulverized. Store in a tightly-covered jar.

For each serving, measure 2 rounded tsp of almond mix into a saucepan. Blend with a little water to make a smooth paste, and add 1/2 cup water for each serving. Bring to a boil and sweeten to taste. (Try 1 tsp sugar per serving.)

STEAMED KUMQUATS

If you do serve a sweet after dinner, this is most appropriate. It's simple and light. Use five kumquats for a serving.

1 lb fresh kumquats
1/4 cup sugar

Place kumquats in a bowl, sprinkle with sugar, and steam them for 20 to 30 minutes, or until soft.

Linda Lew grew up in Chungking where her father was a prominent banker. She first observed the art of Chinese cooking by watching the cooks in her family's kitchen where each course was prepared by a different cook. Since her father loved to entertain, there were two shifts of cooks on the household staff. When Linda was married and living in Taiwan, she kept up her lively interest in food and regional cooking. Now a resident of San Francisco, Linda teaches Northern Chinese cooking—besides cooking for her husband, an engineer, and her two young twins.

Agnes Lee, Linda's older daughter, was born in Taipei and teaches Chinese cooking in Livermore, California. She is married and has a son, Kevin. All of Linda's recipes were co-authored and translated by Agnes.

Elizabeth Brotherton, who compiled the material for this book, has long been a devotee of Chinese cooking. She and her husband **Joe** live on Telegraph Hill in San Francisco with their younger daughter Rose. **Joe Brotherton's** paintings have been exhibited in several museums.

INDEX